The Plays of Lillian Hellman

A Critical Study

To
the loving memory of
my beloved father
Sri T. Babu Rao
who longed to see me a doctor

The Plays of Lillian Hellman

A Critical Study

T. NAGAMANI

PRESTIGE

Published by
PRESTIGE BOOKS
3/28, East Patel Nagar
New Delhi 110 008
e-mail: prestigebooks@greatindian.com

ISBN: 81-7551-102-8

Rs. 400

Composed by Vivek Mathur, Delhi 110 006 Ph. 3981867
Printed at Chaman Offset Press, New Delhi 110 002

Contents

Preface

Hellman's dramatic work has generally been approached as 'well-made play,' 'melodrama' and drama of 'social protest.' If some critics like Eric Bentley give her plays a political label, other critics like Kimball King offer a Freudian interpretation. But, one can hope to gain a fuller appreciation of Hellman's plays by approaching them from a moral point of view. For, Hellman's vision, in the final analysis, seems to be rather moral than social, political, or psychological.

The aim of the present book is to make a close study of Lillian Hellman's plays, with a view to showing that she is a playwright with a deep moral concern. Hellman is strongly moral and she writes with a sense of righteous indignation. Like Shakespeare, she is greatly concerned with evil in society. Her plays explore the corruptive nature of evil and the decay of morally deficient characters. With a highly moral view, she interprets both action and failure in terms of good and evil.

The book is divided into ten chapters based on Hellman's eight original plays. The introductory chapter seeks to show how Hellman emerged as a bright star in the cloudy horizons of the Great Depression, with an overwhelming preoccupation with social issues. It discusses how Hellman, like the major dramatists of the period—Lawson, Rice, Anderson and Odets—is concerned with the political and social issues raised by the Depression and the rise of fascism. It reveals how Hellman was influenced by great dramatists like Ibsen, Brecht and Chekhov to shape herself as a committed playwright, pre-eminently concerned with the moral implications of drama.

The second chapter deals with *The Children's Hour* (1934) in which two headmistresses of a Scottish Girls Academy are falsely accused of homosexual activity. It shows how the play, which shocked many with its almost forbidden theme, is not about lesbianism, but about a lie. It reveals that the play is at once an engrossing drama and a serious study of abnormal psychology, demonstrating as it does the playwright's ability to weave tough-minded expressions of liberal social attitudes into a suspenseful plot.

The third chapter is concerned with Hellman's second play, *Days to Come* (1936), in which she unsuccessfully attempts to incorporate themes regarding the evolving character of labour unions and the conflicts between members of family. The play presents a family of more or less well-intentioned Americans confronted by the problem of dealing with organised labour when their employees undertake a strike. The significance of the play lies in Hellman attempting to develop a theme common to all her plays that the world we live in is the sum total of the acts of each individual in it.

The fourth chapter is devoted to *The Little Foxes* (1938) which depicts greed and sibling rivalry among members of the affluent Hubbard family who seek to expand their wealth by exploiting the cheap labour force available in their community. With its scathing criticism of the vindictiveness and rapacity of bourgeois society, the play is concerned with social degradation and moral decay as inescapable consequences of the inordinate appetite for money and power.

The fifth chapter is about *Watch on the Rhine* (1940) which centres upon a family involved in the anti-Nazi movement. It is a vital, eloquent and compassionate play about an American family suddenly awakened to the danger threatening their liberty. The play asserts the necessity of struggle against both evil and the passivity of bystanders.

The sixth chapter concerns itself with *The Searching Wind* (1944) in which Hellman advocates anti-fascist activity in an examination of well-meaning, affluent Americans who fail to use their money and influence to halt the progress of Mussolini and Hitler. It shows how the play is reminiscent of *Days to Come*, making the point that the world is the sum total of each person's personal actions.

The seventh chapter pertains to *Another Part of the Forest* (1947) in which Hellman returns to the Hubbard family, twenty years prior to the action of *The Little Foxes*, in order to trace the origins of their obsession with money and power. Though the play is not as successful as *The Little Foxes*, it is important for Hellman's fresh insights into the sources of human behaviour.

The eighth chapter relates itself to *The Autumn Garden* (1951) which presents a group of middle-aged individuals, vacationing on the gulf of Mexico, who discover the ramifications of the decisions and compromises they have made. As an unusually introspective work in Hellman's canon, the play draws comparisons to the works of Chekhov for its emphasis on characterization and dialogue.

The ninth chapter deals with *Toys in the Attic* (1960) which is a Southern Gothic piece revolving around the obsessive and destructive relationship between spinster sisters and their younger brother whose sudden wealth and marriage threaten their domination of him. Hellman's mastery of irony makes *Toys in the Attic* both character drama and dark comedy, as it combines all of her earlier virtues as a dramatist with compassion, truth, detachment and tremendous dramatic power.

While offering a summing up of the main argument of the thesis, an attempt is made in the concluding chapter to assess the achievement of Lillian Hellman as a dramatist, highlighting her significant contribution to the development of social drama in the American theatre.

I take this opportunity to express my deep sense of gratitude to all those who helped me in bringing out this book on Lillian Hellman. I am grateful to Professor K. Venkata Reddy, former Professor and Head of the Department of English, Sri Krishnadevaraya University, Anantapur, for his critical remarks and insightful comments which have gone a long way in shaping the book. I am grateful to Professor C.R. Visweswara Rao and other members of the Department of English and Comparative Literature who have helped me as and when I approached them. I express my grateful thanks to Dr. P. Somanath for his timely help.

But for the loving concern of my mother, Smt. Tenneti Indira Kalyani, and my beloved Minu, it would not have been possible for me to undertake this project. I fondly remember and gratefully acknowledge their help. I am deeply beholden to my loving husband, Shri Bhanwar Lal, IAS, but for whose initiative and drive, affectionate care and constant encouragement I would not have been in a position to complete this book. Words fail to express what I intensely feel in my heart of hearts. I remain indebted to him for ever.

TENNETI NAGAMANI

Lillian Hellman and Her Times

> The theatre . . . is a vivid and vibrant expression of truths and ideas. It helps to make life whole.
>
> Brooks Atkinson

The 1930s in the literary world has been considered a great period of revolution and resurgence. The economic depression, the industrial explosion resulting in the growing unrest among workers and the birth of trade unionism, the rise of nationalist movements in colonial countries under imperialistic governments and the exploitation of various kinds resulting in capitalistic societies—these are some of the economic, social and political conditions that affected the literary world bringing about a remarkable change in the attitude of the writers towards life and literature. An editorial of the *London Magazine* pointed out that during the thirties "it was a widely held view that poets, novelists and playwrights should be closely concerned in their writing with the fundamental political and social issues of their time."[1]

Commitment on the part of creative writers had come to assume new literary connotations during this period. Whether they subscribed to the political ideology of Marxism or not, commitment was important to them. As Gerald Rabkin puts it, "whatever his politics, the significant fact is that in the thirties the writer felt compelled to commit himself, to involve himself in the social issues of the age to which he belonged."[2] In *The Writer and Commitment*, John Mander continually asserts the importance of commitment for the writer. "What matters in art," he states, "is the quality and nature of artists' commitment."[3]

The problem of commitment manifested itself most sharply and clearly in the drama of the 1930s since drama, by its very nature, is an immediate and public art. Drama is pre-eminently a 'social art' and has a direct impact on society. As Francis Fergusson has pointed out, "the theatre artist cannot practise his art without real people assembled before a real stage; a theatre without an audience is a contradiction in terms."[4] In an essay entitled "Theatre and Living," Tynan argues that there are three attitudes toward life open to the dramatist: he can record it imitatively, he can withdraw from it, or he can seek to change it. Great art, he continues, must, by definition deal with more than the recording of detail: it must, in the nature of the case, comment, and drama, in particular, demands not only explanation but resolution as well. "Therefore," Tynan asserts, "the artist and particularly the dramatist, is forced to involve himself with political issues, to immerse himself in the world of which he is a part. Art which ignores social questions, is a shrinking flower that conspires at its own death by ignoring the soil in which it grows."[5]

The dramatist of the period, who found a number of burning problems around him demanding immediate attention, began to use the stage as a 'pulpit,' a 'soap-box' and a 'makeshift platform' from which he could shout his own personal solutions to contemporary problems. Dramatists whose medium of communication was the stage, started using the whole machinery of the theatre as "a way of thinking critically and constructively about their world."[6] They came to believe that 'a drama of no comment is a drama of no future.'

Sam Smiley, in his *The Drama of Attack: Didactic Plays of the American Depression*, describes three types of commitment among the social dramatists of the thirties—multiform social concerns, rigid political systems and parties, and leftist theatrical companies. The late twenties and the early thirties saw the formation of several leftist theatrical companies committed to the production of plays of social significance. For instance, the New Theatre League, the Theatre Union and the Group Theatre, were all created for promoting socially relevant drama. They were less concerned with aesthetic quality than with social or political programmes. However, the Group Theatre placed its major emphasis on the combination of social comment and art. As Rabkin puts it, "whatever the final verdict as to the durability of American drama in the thirties, there is no doubt that much of this accomplishment is due to the efforts of the Group Theatre." (86)

Three distinct stages of development are evident in the decade beginning with the first years of the Depression. The first phase, 1929-33, saw attempts at 'hard-line' Marxist drama by such writers as Clarie, Paul Sifton and Elmer Rice and writers of social comedy like Philip Barry and S.N. Behrman. It moved from mild lampooning of mores and convention to biting political satire as is seen in Maxwell Anderson's *Both Your Houses.*

The second phase, 1933-36, saw the advent of the social critics on stage as Marxist and communist didacticians, whose plays such as Clifford Odets's *Waiting for Lefty* and Kingsley's *Dead End* synthesized the elements of agit-prop with the more acceptable forms of Broadway plays to offer a drama which declaimed, exhorted and informed its audience, but entertained it as well. This synthesis continued to influence drama through such companies as the Federal Theatre Project.

The third phase, 1937-39, which began as a softening of the 'hard-line' Marxist position gave way to attempts to synthesize political and social activism with the 'well-made' play such as Odets's *Golden Boy.* The phase came to fruition as Philip Barry's *The Philadelphia Story* effectively combined social comedy and social criticism into a play which illustrated the need for unity and understanding between all elements of American society on the eve of an international crisis.

II

According to Gerald Rabkin, a social drama is a play which suggests social alternatives, "either reformist or radical," or a play which demands "personal or collective action." (78) It is heartening to note that the majority of plays of social consciousness produced during the thirties fulfil Rabkin's requirements of social drama. In these plays, the emphasis shifts from radical cures to careful diagnosis. Instead of examining the relationship between man and God as in messianic drama, the social dramatist concentrates on man in society in conflict with community, government, academy, church or family.

Social drama is mostly written in the realistic or naturalistic style. Messianic voluptuousness and exuberance are replaced by more controlled and modulated feelings, as the playwright absents himself from the proceedings and permits the action to speak for itself. Social, political, moral and economic questions are aired in an atmosphere of impartiality. Psychological insights and scientific ideas are presented without any qualms of conscience.

As for character, social drama puts contemporary society on the stage and draws its 'dramatis personae' from the middle class. The protagonist is subject to the same laws as the audience; shares the same ambitions (or the lack of them); performs the same domestic duties; and speaks the same unlovely prose. Human stature, in other words, shrinks to average height and man's surroundings.

The social drama of the thirties grew from a precocious comedy, gently poking fun at national ills in the late twenties, to a keen satiric comedy by 1933. It had become palatable to audiences because the playwrights learned to use drama effectively as a weapon of social change by making it both inform and entertain the audiences. In other words, it presented social criticism in the form of sugar-coated pills. Although such plays as Anderson's *Both Your Houses* (1933) and Behrman's *Rain from Heaven* (1934) are hardly Marxist in their appeal or message, they are seriously critical of social institutions and prevailing national attitudes concerning self-perpetuating evil of commercial wealth. Though these plays contain 'call to action,' they are couched in well-made dialogue. The design of their social comedy is to create a public arousal through knowledge rather than through the preachings of the political drama of the avowed leftists. What they seek to do is to evoke the 'pleasure and profit' idea of combining a 'sermon' with a 'tickle.'[7]

The development of social drama in the thirties is largely an extension of work of playwrights like Howard Lawson and Elmer

Rice in the twenties who made the theatre "a school, a forum, a communal institution and a weapon in the hands of the masses for fashioning a sound society."[8] In his 'preface' to Ben Blake's *The Awakening of the American Theatre*, Lawson substantiates this point of view and states, "Behind these pages is a story best appreciated, perhaps, by those like myself who have laboured long at the task of establishing this theatre movement. A long road still lies ahead. But history has been made."[9]

One of the most outspoken, socially conscious playwrights of the twenties, Lawson became a leading leftist playwright and critic. Each of his significant plays—*Processional* (1925), *Nirvana* (1925), *Loudspeaker* (1926), *International* (1927) and *Success Story* (1930)—contains sufficient entertainment potential as well as social comment. As R.C. Reynolds puts it "by using expressionistic technique and caricature and satire, Lawson was cunningly able to stage social comment which ideally applied the theory of 'sermon and tickle.'"[10] If Lawson was a mentor to some, he was a model to others. In his plays, he "represents the man who is always conscious of his role in society, of his debt to it and also of its encroachments upon his individual conscience."[11] However promising his work appeared in the late twenties, Lawson's plays became increasingly didactic. It was this growing emphasis on informing the audience at the expense of entertaining them that marked his decline as a successful voice in the drama of the early Depression years.

Elmer Rice reflects his deep concern with the social issues of the times in all his plays. Right from his earliest attempt at playwriting, *A Defection from Grace*, which focuses on the rampant corruption in society and the conflict between a woman's career and her domestic life, till the last published play, *Cue for Passion*, Rice attempts to bring to light the ills afflicting the American society. Elmer Rice is deeply concerned about restoring finer values like human dignity and individual freedom. Through several plays, Rice advocates these values. Rice's most popular play, *The Adding Machine*, is a step in this direction. It has justly been regarded as the best play that vividly portrays the dehumanising effects of the machine. The play presents, "soul destroying drudgery and routine, of grubby passions unsatisfied, of grubbier dreams unrealised, and of the eternal babble of long dead cliches."[12] Elmer Rice, as rightly pointed out by Gerald Rabkin, "suggests the need for rapprochement which would combine the social fervor of Marxism and the individual liberties of capitalist democracy." (253)

The theatre of the thirties is remembered for its playwrights not because they produced masterpieces for the ages, but because they responded to the challenge of their times vigorously and excitingly. Of late, it has become increasingly apparent that the past decade needed their verve, and could have used their passion for engaging themselves to a cause, an ideal or even a delusion.

The dramatists of this period added social commitment to the substance of their plays. They became public spirited, less interested in the problems of the individual and more worried about national distresses. The speed with which they adapted themselves to the new environment differed with each playwright.

The contribution that the playwrights of this generation made to the theatre lay in their ability to discuss all sides of serious issues in a dialogue that argued rather than exhorted. In their plays they reviewed the evidence of social decay without dogmatism and without an attempt to suggest easy cures. The crisp dialogue that in the twenties exposed the personal difficulties within the home became a medium for the treatment of public problems. They wished to analyze the social forces that created killers, perjurers, slanderers and other anti-social beings. By winning sympathy among audiences for their fierce disquisitions on social injustice, they succeeded in sharpening the tone of broadway drama.

III

The playwrights of this 'depression period' can be divided into two main groups. The first group consists of those who first arrived in the theatre—Clifford Odets, Lillian Hellman, Irwin Shaw, Victor Wolfson, Sidney Kingsley and William Saroyan.

These dramatists brought with them a reputation achieved in the previous decade. Their plays were popular less for their showmanship and more for their incorporation of literary themes—naturalism, allegory and social relevance. The other group includes Elmer Rice, John Howard Lawson, S.N. Behrman, Philip Barry, Robert E. Sherwood, Paul Green, and Maxwell Anderson, who emerged later in the dramatic scenario. To these two groups, a third group may be added which consists of very young playwrights, Arthur Miller and Tennessee Williams, whose work first arrived on the professional stage in the 1940s, but whose youth and early writings were formed in the decade of the depression.

However, the characteristic playwriting of the decade was not the exclusive contribution of any single group. The lengthening perspective of history brings the first two playwriting generations of the thirties closer to each other. They were jointly responsible for what was good and bad in the dramatic art of the times—for its passionateness and sentimentality, genuine feeling for common humanity, moral vigour and didactic crudity. The playwriting of the thirties was not a cult but simply playwriting leavened by the authors' engagement to life in the midst of economic and political crisis.

While the nineteen thirties witnessed a virtual hey-day for comedies by Kaufman, Moss Hart and William Saroyan, it also saw the genius of Maxwell Anderson and Clifford Odets who used techniques of showmanship and theatricality in their plays. Because their plays were popular successes, modern critics tend to dismiss them as popular writers rather than to consider them as committed literary artists.

Though he aspired to the empyrean of poetic tragedy, Maxwell Anderson could successfully reflect only the tensions of his time, as in the political satire of *Both Your Houses*, or refract them as in the oblique dramaturgy of *Winterset* and *High Tor*. It is true that Anderson, like many other playwrights of the period, wrote plays about social evils of different kind such as political and social corruption, housing problems and the lack of understanding between people within a social framework. But his approach to such problems in his plays like *Winterset* is different from Odets's approach in *Waiting for Lefty* in that he depicts the problems and dramatises their effects whereas Odets "dramatises the problem and calls for action in a demand for immediate redress."[13]

While Elmer Rice presents the drawbacks in society and calls for a return to the noble values like individual dignity, the credit for calling for collective action goes to Clifford Odets whose work is intricately interwoven with the dislocated strands of American life in the 1930s. He gave voice to the anguish of a generation which was going through one of the worst periods of American history, both socially and economically. He identified himself with the suffering working class and middle class sections of American population and effectively presented the socio-economic problems from their point of view.

In his very first play, *Waiting for Lefty*, Odets presents the striving of worthy young people, the frustration of a generation unable to find security or fulfilment in the Depression period. In *Till the Day I Die*, Odets takes up for presentation the brutalities of Nazi oppression vis-a-vis the high ideals of the communist party and the sincerity of the party comrades. Odets, who considers the family as the basic social unit, portrays the effects of the Depression period on a typical American working class family in *Awake and Sing*. In *Paradise Lost*, he presents a much darker picture of the decaying middle class. The image that pervades the play is the 'sweet smell of decay.'

In *The Golden Boy* and *The Big Knife*, Odets presents the consequences of attaining or attempting to achieve 'success' in the prevailing American sense. The problem of homelessness in all its ramifications is portrayed by Odets in *The Night Music*. The feeling of loneliness, personal isolation and the sense of insecurity prevalent in American society during the 30s is presented in the play through people sleeping in the lobby of hotels, in the parks, and in the constant movement of characters from one place to another. In *Rocket to the Moon*, Odets presents the troubles and tribulations faced by professionals like doctors and personal secretaries in the American society during the thirties. Incidentally he also suggests the importance of love as the invigorating emotion that can sustain human relations during the troubled times.

In *The Country Girl*, Odets takes up for presentation the problems faced by yet another section of the American population—the sensitive artist. The play deals with the re-emergence of Frank Elgin as a talented actor from the abysmal depths into which circumstances have pushed him. The last play of his career, *The Flowering Peach* (1954), can also be seen to reflect the major concerns of the times. During the fifties, because of the bombing of Hiroshima and Nagasaki, there was a growing awareness about the serious disaster that a nuclear war might cause. Odets, in order to reflect this concern, chose as the basis for his play Noah's legend. The disaster caused by the floods in the legend serves admirably to reflect the possible annihilation consequent upon a nuclear war.

Thus, it can be seen that Odets, who wrote plays for more than two decades, reflects in almost every play, the social problems of the times. During the 1930s when the lives of working class and middle class sections of the American population became miserable, Odets used the stage to even advocate collective action. In several plays like *The Golden Boy*, *Awake and Sing* and *Paradise Lost*, Odets deals with the prevalent socio-economic problems and suggests that through determined action, the situation can be rectified.

However, it is generally believed that Odets lost his force as a maker of social drama after *The Golden Boy*. In spite of his attempt to radically alter the intellectual concepts of his audience, Odets was unable to balance his social concerns with his dramatic medium. But, when he softened his social exhortation and political didacticism in favour of dramatic or literary style, many in his audience missed his point. His plays continued to 'work' theatrically but "the verve and drive which had moved the audience at the end of *Waiting for Lefty* or brought them to see *The Golden Boy* and applaud its artistry were gone, and Odets's plays became melancholy and flat without the tonic of commitment he gave them between 1935 and 1937."[14]

It is important to note that during the nineteen thirties, the

American stage finally became more of a playwright's theatre than ever before in its history, "affording incentive to the playwright not to truckle to popular taste, giving him some necessary measure of control over his playscript, and encouraging him to use modern content, argument and idea into his work."[15] Hence the importance of the thirties as a decade from the standpoint of the changing role of the writer from technician to artist.

However, there are also some misconceptions about the period of the thirties, one of the most prevalent being the view that the period was inimical to humour and light entertainment. Nothing could be farther from the truth, even if zealots of 'social drama' seemed to imply that seriousness undermined the American way of life. George Kaufman and his collaborators assimilated the economic struggle quite successfully in their comedies of the depression—*Stage Door* and *You Can't Take it with You*—as did Arthur Kober in *Having a Wonderful Time* and Saroyan in *My Heart's in the Highlands*. And, political tension was also successfully translated into comedy by Maxwell Anderson in *Both Your Houses* and *High Tor* and by Behrman in *Biography* and *End of Summer*. There was a distinct comic strain in the work of Odets, Robert Arday, Marc Blitzstein and others. The vigour of the thirties sustained a frolic as well as a political commitment. No wonder, therefore, if John Mason Brown described this Depression period of the theatre as 'these full lean years.'

Moreover, we must free ourselves of the notion that the characteristic plays of the period were standardized works of sociological realism. The distinctive realism of the thirties was something else. We must distinguish it from merely descriptive realism because it brought factual detail into focus by means of some perspective of thought and feeling. This type of social drama must be distinguished from the ordinary 'problem play' because the dramatist did not offer specific solutions to specific problems so much as he challenged an entire way of life. These plays tended to be revolutionary in spirit rather than ploddingly reformatory and their realism was characterized by intensity and explosiveness. The pathos and fury in the plays of Odets and the sympathy and scorn in those of Hellman were anything but impersonal qualities born of ideology or introduced into the work by ideological persuasion. The characteristic social dramas of the decade brought much resolve and not a little bravura into the theatre. They sought maximum expressiveness for their protest, conviction and compassion. And to expressive language they added an energetic search for expressive form.

For a period full of collectivist idealism, the thirties were curiously rich in individuality, much richer than the fifties, when socialistic idealism had virtually vanished from the theatre. The 'social' dramatists who seemed to share so much anti-capitalist animus and pro-socialist faith were distinct individuals. The poignant singularity of young Odets was often marked. By way of contrast, the young Sidney Kingsley was meticulous and logical. Paul Green was 'regional' yet 'universal,' realistic yet poetic.

However, there was one serious limitation in the playwriting of the period. Many a playwright used social faith as a crutch very much as recent playwrights have used psychopathology. When the crutch slipped from under the armpit, the playwright stumbled. Even Odets's considerable dramatic talent could not consistently sustain him as has already been shown, and less gifted social dramatists crumbled. Lillian Hellman alone continued to create with unabated power.

IV

It would take a strong mind and will to create a play that could combine social statement with entertaining drama. As Odets's plays slipped increasingly into melancholy themes and Lawson and other leftists continued to exhort Marxist philosophy through loosely constructed melodramas, audiences and critics began to look for fresher themes and newer approaches to social problems, Lillian Hellman rose to the occasion to fill the bill and prove her mettle.[16]

Lillian Hellman emerged as a bright star in the cloudy horizons of the Great Depression of the thirties. Beginning in an unprecedented economic dislocation and ending in a global war, the decade was a massive trial of endurance. The decade began with industrial chaos, the collapse of the financial structure, mass unemployment and it ended with Second World War. The social climate of the 1930s brought a new outburst of awareness of the theatre and the theatre became an active participant in the struggle to arouse a disheartened people to renewed optimism. Social protest was in the air which was reflected in the creative thoughts of the time. The result was a good drama which pricked the conscience and stimulated the imagination of the audience.

A more realistic view of mankind's prospects is present in the plays of Lillian Hellman who is widely acclaimed as one of America's most distinguished playwrights. In 1941, Freedlay and Reeves, in *A History of the Theatre*, expressed an opinion which still prevails: "Lillian Hellman has demonstrated greater power than any woman now writing for the stage."[17] She has a permanent place in the American theatre, not just as the first American woman playwright, but as one who could fashion a play with both relevance and drama.

As a playwright of the 'Depression period,' Hellman had the will and impulse to express the age in her plays. Along with many American writers from the generation of the 1930s, the "red decade,"[18] Hellman addressed the 'Great Depression' in her plays of the period and reflected on its aftermath her own political awakening throughout her career. Her analysis of American society is essentially Marxist, since it is based on the primacy of material and economic conditions to explain social relations and emphasizes environmental conditioning conflict among classes, and the hope that a new person, socialist man, would be born of the conflict through the dialectical collision of opposites.

Lillian Hellman is essentially a socially conscious playwright concerned with social and economic justice. Naturally, she was influenced by deeply committed playwrights like Brecht, Ibsen and Chekhov. She never recanted her belief in the visionary goal to which socialism aspires, and she came to admire Brecht as the master dramatist of the century. Although Hellman never speculated about direct influences, a number of resemblances in technique and attitude between some of her later works and certain Brecht's plays can be noted. A more significant influence of Brechtian theory of drama can be noted in her best and most explicitly political plays of the late 1930s. Like Brecht, Hellman expects her audience to be enraged enough by the injustice she dramatizes to leave the theatre and take social action. But, also like Brecht, she has scant faith in the audience's own capacity for moral commitment. Indeed, these resemblances with Brecht make Hellman's own dramatic method appear more sophisticated than critics widely assume and may indicate a generic feature of political drama independent of influences.

Skilfully constructed and nailed together with strong scenes, crisp dialogue and powerful characters, Hellman's theatre is fashioned largely under the influence of Ibsen. Like Ibsen, she believes that drama could be a vehicle for social commentary, psychological insight and, above all, sharp incision into the diseased body of a corrupt society. As her model was Ibsen, she shared his love of tightly knit plots in her early plays. Her best plays, like Ibsen's, are those in which a powerful character cuts loose and transcends the limitations of the play's rigid symmetry and plot contrivance. Hellman's *The Little Foxes*, like Ibsen's *Hedda Gabler* and *A Doll's House*, addresses important social questions.

Later, in her playwriting career, Hellman made a conscientious effort to loosen up her style by employing the more indirect, apparently plotless techniques of Chekhov. However, the traces of Chekhov's influence can be drawn even in her earlier play, *The Little Foxes*, where Chekhov's brilliant depiction of the effete but cultured Russian upper class at the turn of the century is seen in his *The Cherry Orchard* and *Three Sisters*. But, in the later plays like *The Autumn Garden* and *Toys in the Attic*, Hellman turned to Chekhov for inspiration. They recall the mood and ambiguous moral judgements of the Russian dramatist. Neither of these plays has a truly pernicious villain and most of the characters seem to suffer from a Chekhovian paralysis of will. The atmosphere is deterministic and the plots are truer to life. But she never wavered in her Ibsen-influenced conviction that theatre could be a force for change in what she considered an unethical, unjust, essentially venal world.

V

Hellman, in her three Memoirs—*An Unfinished Woman* (1969), *Pentimento* (1973) and *Scoundrel Time* (1976)—gives a new style of writing biography to the American Theatre. In these, she has given readers the meat and left the bare bones for the academics. One can legitimately examine the memoirs for the insights they provide into her dramatic craftsmanship and progress.

The first book, *An Unfinished Woman*, is built as a narrative, not strictly chronological, but still chiefly linear in movement from past to present and back again, relating events and persons to time and to each other. The second, *Pentimento*, is constructed as a series of portraits, each a unit, including group portraits and landscapes. It demonstrates the complete mastery of Hellman's method as vision gives technique and technique reveals vision. The third, *Scoundrel Time*, is a frustratingly slim volume, made thicker by an introduction by Garry Wills, which gives the background of the McCarthy Inquisition for those too young or too forgetful to remember it. What she gives the reader here is a personal, moral history.

There seems to be some differences in the forms of the separate chapters or portraits in *An Unfinished Woman* and *Pentimento*. But that is all deceptive. At first glance they seem to fall into three categories—the cluster of anecdotes or brief reminiscences grouped around a period or a subject, the diaries and the dramatic tales or short stories told dramatically like plays or film scripts. But a closer look reveals that the anecdotes may be clustered to illustrate a theme, and a diary may turn out to be a mysterious quest or a dramatic tale.

As speaker and actress, Hellman is the principal unifier of the memoirs, and recurrent settings and characters also help to unify the books as they did her life. They reveal the author, but in carefully selected times, places and company. Even in the anecdotes and diaries, she is both narrator and protagonist, in a series of short, self-contained dramas.

By the time she wrote *An Unfinished Woman*, Hellman had moved from the impersonal public tone of the early non-fiction to 'dramatic' organization, with herself as the protagonist and viewpoint character. She had mastered the use of sentence and paragraph rhythm to create a mood, convey an attitude. She had developed fully the use of extended metaphor, of the concrete to convey the abstract. Hellman had mastered in the independent sections of the first memoir the techniques of organizing memory and self-analysis in time-whorls around a central figure or image.

The sum of *Pentimento* is more than that of the portraits which are its parts. It gives the reader a portrait of a lady who, while judging others, reserves the severest judgements for herself. The lady's clarity of mind and moral sensibility make readers question themselves, perhaps the best gift a book can give in these times.

Scoundrel Time focuses on a limited period in the national madness that began in the late 1940s and subsided in the late 1950s. Compared to the other memoirs, *Scoundrel Time* is a minor literary performance that elicited a major political controversy. Hellman, in this memoir, points out the connections between the 'Witchhunt' days of Vietnam and Watergate and doubts our ability to remember long enough to avoid doing it all over again.

Scoundrel Time is different from the other two memoirs. Hellman does not let anything deflect the straight, strong narrative drive, what one critic called the 'understated fury.' If *An Unfinished Woman* and *Pentimento* are portraits in oil, *Scoundrel Time* is a black-and-white engraving. Gone are the interior flashbacks and extended metaphors that had become almost a trademark of her style of the previous memoirs. In a short epilogue, Hellman tells the reader that she is still angry at the people, who let McCarthyism happen. She blames McCarthy, Richard Nixon, and the rest of the boys in the band less than the liberals who did nothing to stop them.

Thus, Hellman's memoirs reveal to us both her mind and art.

Because of these memoirs, and the life revealed in these books, Hellman speaks to us with great moral authority. Her work is much more in the tradition of the autobiographical writings of such literary artists as Stendhal in *The Life of Henry Brulard*, W.B. Yeats in his *Autobiography* and Henry James in *A Small Boy and Others*. It was certainly not the best of times. It was perhaps the worst of times, it was a time of scoundrels and sad clowns, but at this time, a Southern lady, Lillian Hellman, risked her material and creative future for simple human decency, shaming those who would do less.

VI

Between 1935 and 1969, Hellman wrote a few 'occasional' non-dramatic pieces, very few compared to the output of such playwrights as Tennessee Williams or Arthur Miller. These few deal primarily with travel and with her visits to Spain during the Civil War and to Russia during World War II. Viewed chronologically, however, even these non-fiction pieces reveal a steady development toward the persona she used in the memoirs.

Out of her trip to Spain came an article for the *New Republic*, "Day in Spain," and several diary excerpts, collectively titled "The Little War" published in *This is My Best*. The Spanish Civil War pieces are objective journalism, after Hemingway. Hellman's emphasis is on observed details rather than on her subjective reaction. With the exception of *A Blonde Lady* in *This is My Best*, the Civil War pieces have the careful, professional style of a war correspondent who only incidentally is a woman and a creative writer.

A Blonde Lady differs from the other pieces in revealing that Hellman has always been a masterful story-teller. The description of a harrowing drive through the Spanish countryside with a dangerously incompetent driver foreshadows the style of the memoirs.

The Kriendler Collection at Rutgers University contains an unpublished Spanish Civil War manuscript entitled *Richard Harding Davis 1938*. The article expresses strong antipathy toward a *New York Times* correspondent named Carney who avoids danger and is sympathetic to the Franco side. Hellman's final war-piece, *I Meet the Front-Line Russians* (1945), filters out her personality. The language is careful, the diction simple, the emphasis on factual detail.

Hellman's non-dramatic pieces are important to know about her own views on theatre and also on the mission of a dramatist. Hellman claims in her memoir, *Pentimento*, that playwrights are quite different from novelists. There is a light that natural dramatist can see on a dark road. This light is a singleness of purpose, the ability to remain focused on one event. The dramatist conducts one search for one answer and rejects whatever distractions might be enjoyed if he were travelling this road in the company of a novelist. In her conversations with Morsha Norman, Hellman says:

> In a good play each detail falls into useful place. The shortest line, and the smallest stage movement, has an end in view and is not used as a trick, or pull fashionable wool over the audience's eyes. To such writers, in whatever field they be, we give our full attention and they deserve it.[19]

In Hellman's view, it is not enough to learn to write for the theatre. A playwright must learn to survive in the theatre. Hellman says that in order to survive in the theatre, the playwright must act with confidence. Ordinarily timidity and stumbling seem like disintegration in the theatre. They are infectious and corruptive to other frightened people. Hellman watched the theatre changing, and she did not like it. She says:

> I think that after *Watch on the Rhine*, much of the pleasant hijinks of the theatre was never to be seen again because the theatre, like the rest of the country, became expensive, earnest and conservative.[20]

Apart from the section in *Pentimento* called "Theatre," Hellman has written about her work only four times in four theatre pieces in her long career. The first is *Back of Those Foxes* (1939) written in connection with the opening of *The Little Foxes*, the second "Author Jabs the Critic," written in a response to Brooks Atkinson's review of *Another Part of the Forest*, the third "Preface and Postscript," written as an introduction to her *Four Plays*, and the fourth is "Time of the Foxes," a reminiscence of the first production, occasioned by the Lincoln Center revival of *The Little Foxes* in 1967. In both "Author Jabs the Critic" and "Preface and Postscript," the style is polished and impersonal, even when Hellman recalls personal details. Hellman defends her plays against the charge that they are 'well-made' and 'melodramatic.' In all these theatre pieces, Hellman's tone is public.

VII

During the 1930s, the predominant themes explored by the women playwrights appear to be mainly social and domestic in which comedy, farce and melodrama were employed. Glaspell, Crothers and Hansberry have contributed significant works to American drama that explicitly or implicitly helped to establish a female tradition in the American theatre. In the early part of the century the insistence upon the truth, the goal of verisimilitude, 'the desire to get closer to the fact' was the dominant chord in the American drama. And women playwrights did not hesitate to portray issues that drew upon the 'facts' of their lives as women. The women's issues were portrayed by them from the point of view of the 'New Woman' as conceived by Ibsen and Bernard Shaw. This prototypical woman, "was unafraid to challenge male decisions and male dominance."[21]

But, unlike Glaspell and Crothers, Hellman does not present what have been termed 'women's issues' as the central focus of any of her plays. However, in her own characteristic style, she does emphasize economic factors. Her women characters are often portrayed against the socio-economic structures that create and perpetuate their roles. Hellman's characters, though personally and morally responsible for their actions, are almost always portrayed within a social framework, their motives rooted in social forces. Hellman does not stereotype women, but rather portrays them as fully defined individuals, shaped by complex political, social and psychological forces.

In the 1930s, she had begun work with Hammett's encouragement on her first play, *The Children's Hour* (1934), which was an immediate success. From then onwards, she wrote seven more plays and four adaptations upto 1960, and she was launched as one of America's outstanding playwrights. Hellman, in many ways, remains the hardiest survivor of the thirties, because unlike Odets, she commands a technique which can survive abrupt changes in the winds of doctrine.

Hellman's three plays of the decade—*The Children's Hour* (1934), *Days to Come* (1936) and *The Little Foxes* (1938)—reflect social concerns. *The Children's Hour* is a paradigm of a well-crafted, as opposed to the merely well-made, play. It is unusually gripping because Hellman takes the act of lying and links it with one of our deepest fears—total loss. By joining them as cause and effect, Hellman makes the lie more pernicious than it actually is. For this play, Hellman chose a situation which had a foundation, in fact, under the title of *Closed Doors* or *The Great Drumsheugh Case*. All that Hellman did was to bring the story upto the twentieth century. It was an instant and complete success which brought fame to the writer.

Hellman's next play, *Days to Come*, was not a success. It is crowded and over-wrought, but it is a good report of rich liberals in the 1930s and of a labour leader who saw through them. Her third play, *The Little Foxes*, deals with the transition from an old to a new South. It is a powerful drama in which an entire society in decay is revealed. The Hubbards are intended to be human beings as well as masters of selfishness. As Bigsby observes, "*The Little Foxes* was produced in which the writer was pressed to declare his or her allegiance in ideological terms. Despite the subsequent attempt by the House Un-American Activities Committee to turn her into an ideologue, and despite the more simplistic assumptions of *Days to Come*, Hellman was never that. Indeed, she took some pride in her refusal to bend her art to the immediate cause. Her model, in that respect, as in others was Chekhov."[22]

By the end of the thirties, however, American drama had assumed a position of some stature in world drama, and it became a recognised force. During the war years of the forties, American plays largely reflected the agony and anger of an aroused people. The major distinguishing feature was psychological interest in man's emotional reaction to war. Both Hellman and Sherwood reacted vigorously to the war in Europe. With her superior control of melodramatic action, Hellman wrote a powerful anti-fascist play, *Watch on the Rhine* (1941). She made an even more serious comment as she ridiculed the previous twenty years of American foreign policy in *The Searching Wind* (1944). *Watch on the Rhine*, which won the New York Drama Critics award is more popular than *The Little Foxes*. It is the most human of Hellman's plays, the warmest and in some ways the most understanding. It is an improbable story about the betrayal of a resistance worker by a cynical German exile. *The Searching Wind* is an attempt to analyze the moral failures which had led to war, the liberal equivocations and the self-concerned tolerance for the intolerant.

Hellman again returned to the Hubbard family of *The Little Foxes* and wrote *Another Part of the Forest* (1947), set in 1880, twenty years before *The Little Foxes* is set. In the second play, she lays great emphasis on the society's ostracizing of the Hubbards and the impulse to get ahead financially to compensate for their loneliness.

In the mid-century, Hellman turned from Ibsen to Chekhov and wrote two other plays—*The Autumn Garden* (1951) and *Toys in the Attic* (1960). These two plays present middle-aged people who come to recognize the bleakness of their lives but find they cannot change it. In *The Autumn Garden*, Hellman insists that people are responsible for their actions and that they are the sum of their choices. *Toys in the Attic*, Hellman's last successful play, focuses on the individual psychologies of characters whose failure to understand themselves is the origin of their pain. One year after the production of *Toys in the Attic*, Hammett died. With the exception of an adaptation, Hellman never wrote another play.

Since Lillian Hellman is a playwright of the thirties, she has sometimes been taken simply as a social playwright. Although there is implicit anti-capitalism in *The Little Foxes* and explicit anti-fascism in *Watch on the Rhine*, she has always been most concerned with personal morality. No one can deny the importance of Hellman's contribution to the modern theatre as an interpreter of the South and as an American artist. Hellman's plays cover three decades in the annals of the contemporary American drama, from the thirties to the fifties—a period of extraordinary interest and great activity.

The following chapters seek to make an indepth study of Lillian Hellman's eight original plays in terms of their thematic concerns and technical virtuosities.

NOTES

1. John Lehmann, qtd. Gerald Rabkin, *Drama and Commitment: Politics in the American Theatre of the Thirties* (Bloomington: Indiana University Press, 1964), p. 13.
2. Gerald Rabkin, p. 14.
3. John Mander, *The Writer and Commitment* (London: Greenwood Press, 1975), p. 211.
4. Francis Fergusson, qtd. Gerald Rabkin, p. 14.
5. Tynan, *Theatre and Living* (London, 1957), pp. 94-95.
6. William Arrowsmit, "A Greek Theatre of Ideas," *Ideas in the Drama*, ed. John Gassner (New York: Columbia University Press, 1964), p. 1.
7. The idea of combining profit and delight in poetic art goes back to the Aristotelian and Platonic debate on matters of philosophy and rhetoric. For a history of the discussion of the idea, see William K. Wimsatt, Jr. and Cleanth Brooks, *Literary Criticism* (New York: Random House, 1957), pp. 91-92.
8. Granville Hicks, et. al. *Proliterian Literature in the United States* (New York, 1935), pp. 261, 264.
9. Cited by Morgon Y. Himelstein, *Drama was a Weapon* (Connecticut: Greenwood Press, 1976), p. 5.
10. R.C. Reynolds, *Stage Left: The Development of the American So-*

cial Drama in the Thirties (New York: Whitston, 1986), p. 10.

11. Gerald Rabkin, *Drama and Commitment*, pp. 128-29.
12. Joseph Wood Krutch, *American Drama Since 1918* (New York: George Brazler, 1957), p. 230.
13. R.C. Reynolds, "Introduction," *Stage Left*. p. xxiii.
14. R.C. Reynolds, p. 122.
15. Gerald Rabkin, p. 78.
16. Lillian Hellman was introduced into the literary world by Dashiell Hammett, who apparently shaped her writing through often caustic and unappreciative criticism. He also seemed to have given direction to her social ideas and leftist sentiments. Hammett had little patience with the didactic, hardline, protest drama of the left and he frequently looked with disdain upon efforts of such writers as Odets to combine social protest and well-constructed drama. This is made clear by Hellman herself when she discusses in her memoirs of the period her impressions of Hammett's politics. (see Lillian Hellman, *Scoundrel Time*) (Boston: Little Brown, 1976), p. 68.
17. George Freedlay and John A. Reeves, *A History of the Theatre* (New York: Crown, 1951), p. 598.
18. Rolf Meyn employed the term 'red decade' to survey social themes in 1930s American fiction but the label has a long history. See Timothy J. Wiles, "Lillian Hellman's American Political Theatre: The Thirties and Beyond," *Critical Essays on Lillian Hellman*, ed. Mark W. Estrin (Boston, Mass: G.K. Hall, 1989), pp. 90-92.
19. "Lillian Hellman's Gift to a Young Playwright," *New York Times*, Section 2, August 26, 1984, pp. 1-7.
20. *Ibid.*
21. Sharon Friedman, "Feminism as theme in twentieth century American women's drama," *American Studies*, Vol. 25-26, 1984-85, p. 74.
22. C.W.E. Bigsby, "Lillian Hellman," *A Critical Introduction to Twentieth Century American Drama*, Vol. I (Cambridge University Press, 1982), p. 282.

Interplay of Good and Evil: *The Children's Hour*

> Between the dark and the daylight,
> when the night is beginning to lower,
> comes a pause in the day's occupations,
> that is known as the Children's Hour.
>
> Longfellow

Taking its title from Longfellow's poem, *The Children's Hour* (1934) dramatises an evil quality in people. It is based on an actual British court case in which two headmistresses of a Scottish Girls' Academy were falsely accused of homosexual activity by a student. The play shocked many with its almost forbidden theme, but suggested very clearly the bold quality of Hellman's approach to drama. It is neither a lesbian play nor even a play about lesbianism as some critics think. As Hellman herself states, the play is really about a lie, "the bigger the lie, the better as always."[1]

Although Hellman contends that the theme of *The Children's Hour* is not lesbianism, it is unconventional enough to cause a stir among the moralists.[2] What Hellman does in the play is to challenge the conventions of a society that destroys those who deviate from its sexual mores. In writing *The Children's Hour*, Hellman could have been influenced by other plays on the subject such as *These Days* by Katherine Clugston which deals with life in a girls' boarding school and an adaptation of Christa Winsloe's German play, *Girls in Uniform* (produced in 1933), just one year before *The Children's Hour*.

The theme of *The Children's Hour*, as the author herself tells us is "good and evil"[3] though some critics contend that the play is concerned with evil only. For instance, Barret H. Clark says: "Rather I believe evil alone, the evil here as in the character of 'Iago' is a kind of unattached and almost meaningless power. It is like a phenomenon of nature, which cannot be eradicated, hardly perhaps even dealt with."[4] The terms, good and evil, however, do not apply to the theme of homosexuality but to that of destructive scandal-mongering 'the smear and the big lie,' and simultaneously to "the power of the old and rich to rob, to despoil others of livelihood and life."[5]

Hellman is concerned with the universal problem of human evil, gossip and scandal mongering[6] which cause unjust punishment. The theme is supported by the revelation of the shocking power of gossip and the diseased nature of evil. The upright people of the world are disclosed as foolish, tragically blundering because of their own self-righteousness and ignorance. As Judith Olauson comments: "The ascendance of the wickedness which springs from the lie of the child is weighed against the descending capacity for the truth to survive. With relentless momentum, deception outbalances truth and the irreparable damage is done to the two main characters."[7]

The Children's Hour is both an engrossing drama and a serious study of abnormal psychology. It demonstrates the playwright's ability to weave tough-minded expressions of liberal social attitudes into a suspenseful plot. It is not primarily a play about the power of society to enforce its normal norms. It is more concerned with the destructive effects of insisting on one's innocence at all costs.

The Children's Hour is, in many ways, Hellman's atypical play. It is set in and around a Country Boarding School for girls run by two friends—Karen Wright and Martha Dobie—who, after years of hard work and sacrifice, have managed to bring the school to a sound financial footing. One of the students, Mary Tilford, creates a lie and wrecks the lives of the two headmistresses. In an attempt to attract attention, she convinces her grandmother, Amelia Tilford, the main financial backer of the school, that the two teachers—Martha and Karen—are lovers. She also coerces her classmate, Rosaile, to back up her accusation. Mary's chief evidence rests on an over-heard conversation between Martha and her aunt, Lily Mortar, during which the pending marriage between Karen and Joe Cardin, Mrs. Tilford's nephew, is discussed. Lily Mortar, a narrow-minded aunt of Martha, is dependent on her. And Martha tolerates her for economic reasons as a teacher in the school. Conscious of her aunt's unfitness, Martha informs her that she must leave the school. The aunt blames Martha's action on the grounds that Dr. Joe Cardin, Karen's fiance, is in the house at the moment. She says:

> I know what I know. Everytime that man comes into the house, you have a fit. It seems like you just can't stand the idea of them being together. God knows what you'll do when they get married. You're jealous of him that's what it is. . . . And it's unnatural just as unnatural as it can be . . you were always like that even as a child. If you had a little girl friend you always got mad when she likes anybody else.[8]

Startled by a noise at the door, Martha discovers some eavesdropping girls, who promptly report what they have over-heard to Mary. To the astounded question of her classmates: "what are you going to tell your grandmother?" Mary replies: "Oh! I'll think of something to tell her." (26) And we have little doubt at that time that she will create a story of lesbianism about her teachers. But Mary, out of context of the over-heard conversation, persuades her grandmother not only to remove her from the school but also to withdraw her financial support, thus bankrupting and closing it.

Hardened by the ignorant repulsions of millions like her, Mrs. Tilford is incapable not only of the shadow of doubt but also of the shadow of pity. Overcome with disgust, she telephones the shocking news to all the mothers she can reach, so that they may hurry their daughters away from the school. All her previous knowledge of the two admirable young women is at once blotted out by the mention of what to her uninformed mind is unpardonable moral depravity. Karen and Martha appear incredulous and, together with the doctor, they insist on questioning Mary. And when Mary's story is finally shaken, she shrieks that it was another girl who saw them. As the girl has been previously terrorized by Mary's threats, she corroborates Mary's vindictive lies. But, determined to be cleared publicly, Martha and Karen inform Mrs. Tilford that they will sue her for libel. Unfortunately, the only one who can explain the over-heard conversation is Mrs. Mortar. As she is fired from the school, she refuses to return to testify on the women's behalf because she is afraid of being involved in a scandal.

When the last act opens, their 'libel' suit has been lost and Karen and Martha have hidden themselves away in a vacant school. They are publicly branded and they feel that wherever they may go they will be pariahs. The doctor, Joe, who is outwardly cheerful, has a plan for their all going to Vienna, where he studied and can get work. But Karen knows how he longs to stay in his hometown with his own practice. And to her bitter grief she knows that in the heart of the man she loves, there lurks a doubt about their lesbian relationship. So, she clearly tells him: "No, Martha and I have never touched each other." (61) But as she is shaken, she feels that he and she can never again have faith in each other and be natural and joyous together. So, she sends him away 'to think this all over,' although, she is convinced that their relation is at an end.

It is Martha, however, who is the real victim of the tragedy. Whether she has been shocked by her experiences into a clarifying knowledge of her true nature, or whether she has been so shattered as to believe herself abnormal, Martha now confesses to Karen that she does love her. Feeling that she ruined Karen's life and her own, and above all, that they can no longer stay together, Martha steps quietly into the next room and shoots herself.

A few moments later, Mrs. Tilford herself appears at the school. She has come to tell them that Mary was finally compelled to confess her diabolical lies and that her grandmother is there then to make amends including a public apology. But Martha is dead and Karen finds no reason to live. Yet, when she sees the remorseful woman, Karen's bitterness towards her subsides. She understands that Mrs. Tilford, who is herself a victim of society's ignorance, could not have acted otherwise. Finally, she promises not only to accept her help, but even to go back to the doctor later. As the play ends, "we are left with the consolation that Karen will find her way out of this nightmare of medieval torture into a life and love enlarged by new understanding."[9]

The Children's Hour basically presents the conflict between vice and virtue. Karen Wright and Martha Dobie are not women of simple virtue for Martha confesses that Mary's accusations have made her realise that she may be a potential homosexual. Nevertheless, they are presented as relentlessly as any of the virtuous heroines. Mary Tilford is the symbol of vice, for she is completely evil, not only in her malice toward her teachers but also in her persecution of Rosaile, one of her schoolmates, whom she terrorizes because Rosaile has stolen a bracelet. To prevent Mary's exposing her as a thief, Rosaile, although unwilling to do so, finally blurts out the shocking lies which Mary forces her to tell. Thus, "Miss Hellman emphasizes the effect of the malicious slander to make audiences sympathize with the helpless teachers who are ruined by a vicious child."[10]

The relationship between Martha and Karen is drawn with sympathy, perhaps because of Hellman's own experience in her life. As C.W.E. Bigsby states: "And though it is usual to disavow any connection between Lillian Hellman and her characters, her story of Julia, a childhood friend contained in *Pentimento* (1974)—a story which she had found herself unable to tell until then—suggests the origins of this friendship which trembles on the brink of something else. Like her characters in *The Children's Hour*, she too had been accused in public of having such a relationship."[11]

Hellman considers the relationship between the two feminine characters on social and psychological levels. Once college friends, Karen and Martha, are now colleagues in self-made positions of authority. In placing two women in such positions and by forcing the action against them, Hellman is indicating her point of view and exposing a social prejudice that women in authority have always been vulnerable to slander. In this position, as victims of society which can be blinded by implacable evil forces, the characters, emotionally and mentally, take a tragic stature. As Judith Olauson points out, "the two women seem to personify Hellman's view of the hopeless struggles of human beings who contend against evils, as well as the unresolved incompatibilities of human nature, particularly women's nature with society."[12] Supporting this opinion, the *Literary Digest* stated "that there had not been in the theatre in years any two characters more tragic than the two teachers whose lives are ruined as a result of the evil brought on by such an unlikely source."[13]

The rancorous structure of interpersonal relationships in *The Children's Hour* is patterned after the structure of human association in the Venice of Shakespeare's *The Merchant of Venice*. The Victim-Victimizer syndrome in which each victimizer in turn, is reduced to the position of victim is finally shown to be self-destructive. Hellman develops three relationships which are characterized by the circular form and destructive content of the victim-victimizer syndrome: (i) Karen Wright—Mary Tilford (ii) Martha Dobie—Lily Mortar and (iii) Amelia Tilford—Karen Wright/Martha Dobie.

Karen Wright's treatment of Mary Tilford has never been sensitively evaluated. No one has noticed that immediately preceding their initial confrontation, Hellman suggests that Karen is, perhaps, not as compassionate as a teacher of young children should be. For, when Mrs. Mortar complains that one of her students does not 'appreciate' Portia's plea for mercy, Karen replies: "Well I didn't either. I don't think I do yet." (10) The harshness of her discipline demonstrates this truth.

Mary Tilford's offence is a minor one. She attempts to excuse her tardiness by saying that she was picking flowers for Mrs. Mortar. The flowers, Karen knows, were 'picked' from the top of the garbage can, and Mary's stubborn refusal to admit the truth convinces Karen that she must be punished.

Karen: Well, there doesn't seem to be any other way with you; you'll have to be punished. Take your recreation periods alone for the next two weeks. No horse back-riding and no hockey. Don't leave the school grounds for any reason whatsoever. Is that clear?

Mary: Saturday, Too?

Karen: Yes.

Mary: But you said. I could go to the boatraces.

Karen: I'm sorry, but you can't go. (11-12)

These restrictions and punishment may not be of extreme deprivation for an adult but they are so for a child. Mary rightly feels that she is being persecuted. From wanting to tell her grandmother: "how everybody treats me here and the way I get punished for every little thing I do," (12) she moves to a sense of her inner agony. Objectified in her hysterical 'heart problems,' and finally to a rebellious attitude: "They can't get away with treating me like this and they don't have to think they can." (26) Mary accuses Karen and Martha of lesbianism and persists in her lie. Her behaviour is ugly but has been provoked by Karen's earlier ugliness. She seeks an eye for an eye, a tooth for a tooth.

Like Karen, Martha is also not free from certain drawbacks. Karen's inability to deal compassionately with Mary Tilford is parallelled in Act I by Martha Dobie's attitude towards her aunt Lily. Karen and Martha decide that she must be relieved of her teaching duties and literally thrown out of school. Their decision is just, for Mortar is a nuisance and also incompetent. Yet they do not consider for a moment the effect such a dismissal may have on an old woman whose life has been the school. Again, justice is untempered by mercy and Hellman emphasizes the rigidity of the decision's administration. Martha not only tells Lily Mortar that she must leave but also makes fun of her: "We don't want you around when we dig up the buried treasure," and threatens: "You ought to be glad I don't do worse." (17) Mortar pathetically attempts to save face: "I absolutely refuse to be shipped off three thousand miles away. . . . I shall go back to the stage. I'll write my agents tomorrow." (17-18) Everybody knows that her agents are only imaginary and she is really pleading for mercy. As Karen isolates Mary, Martha exiles Lily Mortar. Lily's reaction is the same as Mary's: "You always take your spite out on me." (18)

As she exits, she casts towards Martha a 'malicious half smile' and the malice of revenge is realised when she refuses to clarify the over-heard conversation which will free Karen and Martha from the scar of lesbianism.

Karen and Martha suffer an ironic reversal of fortune: the victimizers become victims themselves. Amelia Tilford, an influential figure in the community of Lancet, misuses her authority over Karen and Martha, just as surely as they had taken advantage of the weaker positions of Mary and Lily. When Mary tells Amelia, that her two teachers are lesbians, the dowager immediately phones the parents of the children who are enrolled at the Wright-Dobie school, and repeats the charges, thus destroying the reputation of the school. When Karen and Martha come for an explanation, Amelia makes it clear, that she does not want these two lepers in her house: "I don't think you should have come here . . . shall not call you names and I will not allow you to call me names. It comes to this. I can't trust myself to talk about it with you now or ever." (44) Her condescension and her revulsion in the face of her visitors's suspected abnormality pervades the scene: "This—this thing is your own. Go away with it. I don't understand it and I don't want any part of it." (45)

Ironically, Karen and Martha now suffer from the same humiliation and ostracism that they so rigorously inflicted on others—Mary and Lily. Thus, Hellman makes the ironic parallel and the lesson even more explicit. Karen and Martha think that they are being unjustly persecuted:

> What is she trying to do to us?
> What is everyone doing to us? (44)

Both feel spiritual agony: "You are not playing with paper dolls We're human beings see? It is our lives you are fooling with. Our lives." (44)

Finally, they feel the need for revenge: "What can we do to you [Amelia]. There must be something—something that makes you feel the way we do tonight. You don't want any part of this. You said. But you'll get a part. More than you bargained for." (45-46)

Clearly, Hellman implies that when one mistreats another, he plants the seeds of his own destruction. Hellman presents a change in the relationships in Act II, but not a change in the structure of relationships. The rancorous victim-victimizer syndrome is as pervasive in this act as it was in the previous one, the difference being that relationships have now come to a full circle.

In the third act, this insight is made even more explicit when Martha admits to herself that she has always been physically attracted to Karen: "It's funny, it's all mixed up. There's something in you and you don't know it. Suddenly a child gets bored and lies and there you are seeing it for the first time. . . . It all seems to come back to me. In some way I have ruined your life. I've ruined my own. I didn't even know." (66) Karen is shaken by the confession, weeps and unconsciously in the Shakespearean manner suggests Martha's fate: "Go and lie down Martha, you'll feel better." (66)

Martha goes and a few minutes later, a shot is heard. She has committed suicide. Martha's attitude towards herself is just as it had been towards others—or as Amelia Tilford's attitude had been towards lesbianism. Indeed, Martha's rancorous attitude towards the imperfections of others is but a reflection of her own self-condemnation. In the words of D.V. Falk: "If the villiany of Mary was, to Hellman, like that of Iago, then the suicide of Martha, in her self-condemnation for what she could not help was like that of Othello, who could not live with what he had seen in himself." (4)

As in the other two acts, there is a parallel action, but this time, it is the difference that is instructive, not the similarity. Martha's self-condemnation is matched by a new found self-disgust in Amelia Tilford. Amelia discovers that Mary has lied about her two teachers and realizes that her hasty phone calls have destroyed two people who are innocent of the charges and even leads one to commit suicide. Her discovery propels her into the same kind of guilt and self-laceration that we have just seen driving Martha to suicide. Amelia begs Karen to allow her to 'do something' for her so that she can in part expiate her sin. Karen accepts Amelia's atonement—and thereby extends compassion—the ultimate good in the world of the play.

Hellman counterpoints Karen's new-found benevolence with the by-now-familiar infantile hostility of Lily Mortar who protests against Amelia Tilford even setting foot in the school: "With Martha lying there? How can you be so feelingless? . . . I won't stay and see it. I'll never let that woman . . ." (68)

Martha's suicide, however, has for Karen been both harrowing and educative. Because of it, she is, she tells Amelia: "Not [young] any more." (70) The brief statement implies that she feels sad at the loss of her own innocence but also suggests that Martha's death has introduced her to a new maturity. Her horror at the guilt that caused Martha's suicide leads her to sympathise with the plight of guilt-ridden Amelia. So, Karen shows mercy on Amelia by accepting her atonement:

Mrs. Tilford: You'll be all right?
Karen: I'll be all right, I suppose. Good-bye, now.
(They both rise. Mrs. Tilford speaks, pleadingly).
Mrs. Tilford: You'll let me help you? You'll let me try?
Karen: Yes, if it will make you feel better.
Mrs. Tilford: (with great feeling) Oh, yes. Oh, yes. Karen.
(Karen walks toward the window)
Karen: (suddenly) Is it nice out?
Mrs. Tilford: It's been cold (Karen opens the window slightly, sits on the ledge.)
Karen: It feels very good. (They smile at each other). (71)

Karen has destroyed the vicious circle that has characterized human relations. Her compassion is the ultimate good in the world of the play.

Thus, *The Children's Hour* deals with malicious gossip that accuses two women of an unnatural relationship and brings in its wake the wreck of their personal lives retaining all the suspensive drive it initially had. It is a striking example of a vital play with considerable merit as a piece of playmaking. It is a tightly constructed play with a good beginning, a middle, and an end. Beginning with Mary Tilford's malicious lie, the play reaches climax with Martha's suicide and ends with Amelia's confession and atonement of her guilt.

But critics like Bentley feel that the structural unity of *The Children's Hour* is marred by the telling of two conflicting stories at a time—"the first is a story of heterosexual teachers accused of lesbianism: the enemy is a society which punishes the innocent. The second is a story of lesbian teachers accused of lesbianism: the enemy is a society which punishes lesbians."[14] He feels that Hellman supposedly established the premise that the two women were 'innocent' and then shifted ground by making one of them 'guilty.'

Just as it is difficult to fall in line with T.S. Eliot's view that Hamlet is 'an artistic failure,' because the focus of the play is divided between Hamlet's taking vengeance on the death of his father and his obsession with his mother's guilt, it is difficult to agree with Bentley's view that *The Children's Hour* is a play which tells two conflicting stories because Hellman carefully prepares her audience in act I for Martha's final revelation. Martha is portrayed as depressed and "fearful" at the prospect of Karen's marriage. Moreover, in Hellman's source '*Bad companions*' the author-editor, William Roughead, had declared emphatically that his interest in the case resides in the fact that the charge was false.

Also, the structural unity of *The Children's Hour* is said to be greatly affected by the third act which is considered an unnecessary intrusion into the play. The third act in general and the final scene in particular have come in for a good deal of criticism. Some contemporary critics fault them on various grounds. To cite but a few instances, Joseph Wood Krutch feels that while the first two acts are powerful and increasingly gripping, the third act is "so strained, so improbable and so thoroughly boring that the effect is almost completely destroyed."[15] Laufe Abe comments that the play must have ended before the final scene. He says that "this weak and ineffectual offer of restitution cannot undo the harm already done."[16] C.W.E. Bigsby observes that "the manner in which the final scene is contrived works against the conclusion."[17]

Thus, some critics feel that the play should have ended with the gunshot and that all that follows it ruins the effect of Hellman's social statement. Interestingly enough, Hellman herself subscribes to this view. She explains why she does so:

> The play probably should have ended with Martha's suicide; the last scene is tense and overburdened. I knew this at the time, but I could not help myself. I am a moral writer, often too moral a writer and I cannot avoid, it seems, the last summing up. I think that is only a mistake when it fails to achieve its purpose, and I would rather make the attempt and fail than fail to make the attempt.[18]

If Hellman feels that the last act is necessary for moral reasons, some other critics too defend it for various other reasons. For instance, R.C. Reynolds feels that "to have left the audience unaware of Mrs. Tilford's discovery of Mary's treachery might not have achieved the complete despair which marks the last act."[19] Philip M. Armato notes that "the conclusion of the play is a structurally necessary resolution, not a tedious reiteration of previous materials."[20] Barret H. Clark observes that the last summing up of Hellman is necessary lest the play be reduced to a sense that "here is evil and make best use of it."[21] George Jean Nathan subscribes to the view that the last scene is necessary for the play. He says: "What Miss Hellman has written down is essential to the integrity of her theme, even if in stage practice it be discommodious to an audience's patience."[22]

However, the real justification for the third act seems to lie in an application of Francis Fergusson's discussion of dramatic rhythm in *The Idea of a Theatre.*[23] He identifies the movements of a realistic play—movements from purpose to suffering and from suffering to new insight—with the protagonist on a search for his true human condition. Examining Ibsen's *Ghosts*, Fergusson finds his rhythm truncated by its abrupt ending because of the lack of the catastrophe. The ending of *The Children's Hour* also prevents a similar truncation. Martha's suicide is the end of her quest, but Karen and Mrs. Tilford must acquire a new insight as a result of that suicide. Thus, because of the final scene, there is acceptance, and the rhythm is complete. Therefore, the last summing up is necessary to *The Children's Hour* which is written in the tradition of Ibsen's realistic drama.

So, like *The Wild Duck*, *The Children's Hour* ends not with a suicide but with a brief discussion on the issues that led to the suicide. Thus, the third act is crucial in that it turns the play from a sub-Ibsen account of integrity assailed by private and public self-interest into a drama about the repression of truth on a number of levels—naturalistic and moral.

Once we agree that the last act is completely necessary, we can easily understand why many of the reviews of the original production of *The Children's Hour* comment that the third act seemed anti-climactic, though well-written. Misled by the impact of the Mary-centred dialogue, they misunderstood the playwright's purpose. The play is not about a psychopathic child or about lesbianism as subject or theme. The subject is character assassination and the theme is the damage done in our world by the so-called 'good' people through self-righteous judgement, selfishness and blindness to their own weaknesses. What we have to bear in mind is that the havoc is created not by Mary's lie, but by the adult-reaction to it, even finally, that of good old Joe, whose doubt topples the last domino. His doubt is the last in a chain of events causing Martha's suicide. Once the child's lie is released on the world, the liar ceases to matter. Thus, properly approached, *The Children's Hour* comes to us as a well knit play with a structural unity of its own.

The Children's Hour is distinguished not only by its structural excellence, but also by its superb art of characterization. The most notable character in the play is Mary Tilford on whom the whole of dramatic interest is centred. Hellman has drawn her character so brilliantly that she seems to be the sole concern of the audience. Once she enters the play with a petty lie on her lips, she dominates the first two acts with her plots and inverted craft as well as with her mad dissembling.

Mary Tilford is presented essentially as a perverse child and a vicious maid. She is drawn with brilliant understanding of the vagaries of a child's nature. Her capacity for lying is tremendous. Her cruelty and sadistic leadership are captivating. Small wonder, therefore, if Mary is considered to be a 'Satanic child' and 'a poisonous young viper,' whose whole disordered life is devoted to cruelty, falsehood and appalling mischief. As Atkinson observes, Mary is "a miniature genius of wickedness."[24]

An orphan under the guardianship of an indulgent grandmother, Mary makes the days of her schoolmates hideous with horrible deeds of evil. She traps them in childish thefts and thereafter enslaves them through threats of exposure. She takes their money, the pitiful little allowances sent by their parents, and she bullies them when they revolt and refuse further to be hurt by her. This type of child magnifies all discipline into the shape of injustice. Thus, when punished for a small fraud and threatened with further thwarting of her demoniac acts, she runs away and goes back to her grandmother, and invents a monstrous accusation against her teachers. The grandmother, first, is contemptuous, but the sly, forceful brat becomes so hysterical that the old woman virtually is browbeaten into belief.

At first, Martha, Karen and Joe regard Mary's behaviour as childish capriciousness and petulance, but they are unaware of the fear which Mary inspires in the other girls. By the time they realize how dangerous and disturbed the child is, it is too late for anyone to believe them. Later, however, when Mrs. Tilford realizes how evil Mary really is, Karen repeats that something is 'wrong' with the girl and that she should be sent away, but for Mrs. Tilford, the presence of her grand-daughter will serve to remind her of her guilt. Mrs. Tilford tells Karen: "No, I could never do that, whatever she does, it must be to me and no one else. She's . . . she's . . ." Karen finishes for her: "Yes, your very own, to live with the rest of your life." (70)

Mary can also be considered an allegorical character. On one level she is a child who imitates the wrong role model in her elders, but she carries that imitation so far as to come to represent pure evil. But, on another level, Mary symbolizes something more than simply a particularly evil child who uses violence and threats to get her way. She also stands for something pernicious in society, an element which is innocently disguised as 'right,' but, in reality is utterly destructive. As R.C. Reynolds points out, Mary can "spread suspicion and destroy anyone or anything she wants to in the name of morality."[25]

However, Mary Tilford, cannot be dismissed as a mere malevolent character as some critics have done by comparing her to Shakespeare's Iago, who is traditionally considered to exemplify 'motiveless malignity.' For instance, an anonymous critic in *Literary Digest* says: "In all reasonableness, there has not been a more malevolent character in the theatre in years than this twelve year old marplot."[26] C.W.E. Bigsby also feels that Mary represents 'simple malignity' which "functions rather too unambiguously in the play, a malevolence which exists not so much as a psychological truth, as an image of implacable hostility which is then compounded by those incapable of conceiving the existence of pure evil."[27]

Perhaps, a better way of looking at Mary's character is to regard her as a neurotic, adolescent girl. This is borne out by Hellman herself, when at the 1952 revival of *The Children's Hour*, she wrote of Mary:

> On the stage, a person is twice as villainous as, say in a novel. When I read that story I thought of the child as neurotic, sly, but not the utterly malignant creature which playgoers see in her. I never see characters as monstrously as the audiences do—in her case I saw her as a bad character but never outside life. It's the results of her lie that make her so dreadful.[28]

Yet another character who closely resembles Mary Tilford is Lily Mortar, aunt of Martha Dobie, who is a consummate liar and fake. She tells the girls long fabrications about her successful theatrical career. She also feels unwanted and out of place in the school knowing that she lives off Martha's largesse, and that she really cannot make her own way in the theatre or elsewhere. She exhibits her unhappiness through malicious accusations eliciting a reply from Martha at one point: "Aunt Lily, the amount of disconnected unpleasantness that goes on in your head could keep a psychologist busy for years." (18) Another time, her niece tells her: "When you're at your best, you're not for tender ears." (18)

Lily Mortar's references to her past glories as an actress, to Sir Henry Irving, to the Infant phenomenon, to the toilet backstage in Rochester, give us a concrete image of her character. And like Mary when she is offstage, she is the subject of discussion between the two teacher friends.

The characterization of the two teachers—Karen Wright and Martha Dobie—who are the victims of Mary Tilford and Lily Mortar, is built more slowly. Interestingly enough, most of their conversation tells us more about Mary and Lily Mortar than about themselves. However, the teachers finally become realized characters for us in the third act, where we finally see them as individuals talking not about Mary or Lily, but about themselves and their lives and their feelings, particularly the dialogue between Karen and Martha and Karen and Mrs. Tilford.

Martha: What is it Karen?
Karen: What are we going to do? It's like that dark hour of the night when half awake you struggle through the black mess you've been dreaming. Then, suddenly you wake up and you see your own bed or your own nightgown and you know you're back again in a solid world. But now it's all the night-mare, there is no solid world. Oh! Martha, why did it happen. What happened? What are we doing here like this?
Martha: Waiting.
Karen: For what?
Martha: I don't know. (55)

Perhaps, the causes for Hellman's rage, the results of which manifest themselves in the characterizations of Martha and Karen, are to be found in the social injustice brought about by the prejudicial and circumstantial evidence which has condemned the two women. The grounds for belief in the allegations are flimsy but, nonetheless, believed first by the town, then by friends and finally by the two women themselves. Martha, like Shakespeare's Othello, pronounces a pathetic judgement on herself and shoots herself.

Although Mary is the initiating force of evil in the play, other characters execute her purposes by their own pride, weakness and gullibility. The most important of such characters is Amelia Tilford, Mary's wealthy grandmother, who is rigid, self-righteous, and status-conscious. The problem with this old woman is two-fold: she is rich and she is old, a member of a generation used to having its own way of creating its own truths. The ending of the play reveals the extent of her power.

Thus, in *The Children's Hour*, Hellman makes every character defeat herself or himself either physically or metaphorically. Martha commits suicide; Karen becomes a wasted person, who will always live with the suspicion that others will have for her; Joe loses Karen's love and trust; Mrs. Tilford loses self-respect; Mary will grow up into an adult who can never be trusted; and Mrs. Mortar, who returns just in time for Martha's suicide, loses her single opportunity to prove herself worthy of trust and affection by refusing to testify. Even the minor characters lose significantly: Agatha, Mrs. Tilford's maid and a surrogate mother for Mary, cannot ever again love or trust the child, and Mary's classmates lose the school where they were happy in their studies.

Like Bernard Shaw's *St. Joan*, Hellman's *The Children's Hour* has often been called a melodrama. Those who have considered the play a melodrama generally see Karen Wright and Martha Dobie, the two teachers, as 'good' characters who are victimized by the 'evil' student, Mary Tilford. To Barret H. Clark and Brooks Atkinson, Mary Tilford is a 'monster.' Hellman's most perceptive critic, Jacob H. Adler, calls Mary "the embodiment of pure evil."[29] If *The Children's Hour* is the story of a sweet little teacher done to death by a tyrannical child, then we must concur with Barret H. Clark's reading of the play's ultimate meaning as: "here is evil . . . make best use of it."[30]

Hellman herself has defended *The Children's Hour* against the attacks of those critics who have labelled it a melodrama. She says that it is wrong to view her characters as being entirely good or evil: "You have no right to see your characters as good or bad. Such words have nothing to do with people you write about. Other people see them that way." Again, in a reply to a question, Hellman says: "Goodness and badness is different from good and bad people isn't it?"[31] So, Hellman's assentations suggest that she did not intend to portray a melodramatic conflict between two 'good teachers' and an 'evil child' when she wrote *The Children's Hour*.

Hellman in *The Children's Hour* offers more than is usually meant by melodrama. As Doris Falk points out, Hellman's plays "are always about good and evil, and evil may seem to prosper unjustly, but the actions and the striving of the characters have meaning and consequence." (44) The moral assumptions, against which Martha and Karen fruitlessly struggle, manifest themselves as one single abstraction—the 'big lie.' And the ultimate defeat of these characters, with each attempt seemingly increasing the strength of the force, makes them play the roles of tragic heroines of, what Krutch calls, 'Modern Drama,' that is protagonists who are defeated by the moral assumptions of society. So, *The Children's Hour* may be said to be closer to tragedy than any other play of Hellman.

One reason that *The Children's Hour* is closer to tragedy than most of the other plays of Hellman is that the evil motivation of Mary and the psychological drives of Martha are both outside the immediate, logical human understanding and control. But it is clear that these forces are allowed to triumph by human machination and the human weakness. Mary Tilford is the first of the despoilers—the foxes who 'spoil our lives'—and her accomplices in evil are the self-righteous Mrs. Tilford and the cowardly Mrs. Mortar.

The tragic dimensions of *The Children's Hour* have been

perceived by both critics and creative writers alike. To cite but a few instances, the anonymous reviewer of *Literary Digest* feels that Karen and Martha are the most tragic characters in the American theatre in the recent past. In their insightful reviews of *These Three*, the first film adaptation of *The Children's Hour*, Alistair Cooke praises the adaptation for its Aristotelian effects. The world famous novelist, Graham Greene, writing in *Spectator*, speaks of its realistic representation of 'nothing less than life.'

To enhance the tragic intensity of *The Children's Hour*, Hellman makes use of dramatic devices like blackmail which is an Ibsenite influence. If Hellman uses blackmail more often than Ibsen, she uses suicide less—only once, and that too in *The Children's Hour*. On the other hand, there is one murder in each of her next three plays—*Days to Come*, *The Little Foxes*, *Watch on the Rhine*. The blackmail in *The Children's Hour* is, in some respects, at least as various as in Ibsen. Mary Tilford intimidates one of her schoolmates into supporting her vicious, destructive lie by threatening to reveal the other child's petty thievery if she does not comply.

Hellman uses blackmail for different dramatic and moralistic purposes when compared to Ibsen. In Ibsen, it is the naive who are blackmailed. In the Hubbard plays—*The Little Foxes* and *Another Part of the Forest*—blackmail is crucial to the turning of the tables. In *The Children's Hour*, Rosaile Wells is a pathetic child, who is little more than an instrument since without her some sort of corroboration of Mary's slander would not have the necessary effect. The blackmail is another example of Mary's destructive evil, her urge to tyrannize. But its primary purpose is as a plot necessity to be defended only on the assumption that in a girls school, there is almost certain to be some misbehaviour open to blackmail.

What further contributes to the tragic intensity of *The Children's Hour* is the way Hellman links social passivity with moral disguise. Hellman dismantles in the play the social stereotype of passivity in Aunt Lily Mortar. Early in the play, the decaying exactress Lily Mortar is over-heard calling the relationship of the headmistress of a school 'just as unnatural as it can be.' Her words, distorted by Mary Tilford, bring about the suicide of one of the women. By shrewdly calculating the cliche of social passivity, Mary blackmails and manipulates both her grandmother and a fellow student into the character assassination of Karen and Martha. She engineers her 'great awful lie' into acceptable truth by exaggerating a social stereotype.

In the course of the play, Aunt Lily Mortar makes a career out of absence, omission and inadvertence. For Lily, the natural thing is the socially customary. Courtesy for her is a mere matter of breeding and passivity, an unconscious and uncritical way of life. In the play's opening scene, Lily and the school girls are involved in a 'great show of doing nothing.' Haphazard sewing and basting complement the fake social graces. Theatrics replaces the candor of labour. Unwittingly, Lily herself points out the description by calling their labours simply women's 'tricks.'

Perhaps, the most 'critical metatheatrical moment' in this opening scene is Lily's hammy reading of Portia's 'Mercy' speech from Shakespeare's *The Merchant of Venice*. On Lily Mortar's lips, these celebrated lines dwindle into a mere elocutionary exercise just as the truth she utters, central to the outcome of the action, is but an over-heard perception. But ironically, it is the three lines that Lily omits which seem to anticipate the outcome of the dramatic action of *The Children's Hour*: "therefore, Jew/Though justice be thy plea, consider this/That in the course of justice none of us/Should see salvation."[32]

Moreover, Lily's verbal omissions in the first scene foreshadow her crucial absence when Karen and Martha need her witness for their trial. Lily's words in the form of 'muttered asides' emerge only indirectly as uncanny truths about the other characters. Lily's comment, 'one master passion in the breast . . . swallows all the rest,' accurately describes Mary's maliciousness.

Just as metatheatrics permits moral disguise in Lily's incomplete Portia and Mary's failed inquisition, so too does it become a metaphor for other forms of playing in *The Children's Hour*. Even structurally, the play subtly suggests the deceptive. All the truth revealing scenes are interrupted so that the continuous action of dramatic unravelling and revelation are missing from the play. By such a sleight of structure, Hellman shifts the focus from blackmail, extortion, and lesbianism to the business of redefining the moral possibilities by giving a dramatically central role to the incidental revelations of Lily Mortar. At the same time, she mocks social passivity by linking it with moral disguise in both Lily and Mary Tilford.

As in Shakespeare's tragedies, irony widens the tragic dimensions of *The Children's Hour*. Although Hellman makes less use of irony in *The Children's Hour* than in her later plays, she makes the most of it by positing mercy as an ultimate good and merciless cruelty as an ultimate evil. She clearly indicates this in the opening lines by quoting from Shakespeare's *The Merchant of Venice*: "It is twice blest: it blesseth him that gives and him that takes." (5) Here, the reference, of course, is to mercy singularly lacking in those who implement the destruction of others. It is not until the curtain falls on *The Children's Hour* that one realizes the irony of the opening lines.

The missing bracelet provides the ironic denouement necessary for the tragic effect of the play. In many of Hellman plays, the plot hinges on a trivial object: a pen knife (*Days to Come*), a medicine bottle (*The Little Foxes*), a briefcase (*Watch on the Rhine*). In *The Children's Hour*, it is a bracelet. At first, Karen's reference to a missing bracelet seems almost gratuitous. Then, when Karen and Martha have almost succeeded in refuting the charge, Mary claims it was not she who saw them together but Rosaile Wells, stressing the fact that it was on the same day that a student's bracelet disappeared. Rosaile, who stole the bracelet, corroborates the lie. A bracelet leads a frightened child to testify against her teachers. It is the same bracelet that provides the ironic denouement when Rosaile's mother discovers it among her daughter's possessions. But it is too late for redress. Martha has committed suicide and Karen has lost her fiance.

Thus, Hellman's maiden attempt as a playwright proved to be a great success as *The Children's Hour* was received well by the critics. The critics of the 1950s understood the theme of *The Children's Hour* and spoke of its contemporary relevance and sometimes applied it specifically to the McCarthy Witchhunt.[33]

They used such phrases as the 'brutal impact of false testimony,' 'exposure of the evils of character assassination,' 'impelling psychological story of the havoc a lie can cause.' Brooks Atkinson thought that the play "might have grown a bit in stature since we have learned that lives can be destroyed by other types of slander. Having been intelligently written for the values of 1934, *The Children's Hour* fits the world of today just as accurately."[34]

John Gassner, the well-known drama critic, has a special word of praise for the play, stressing its importance in the American theatre: "A critic must develop a special resolve to denigrate American drama before he can resist the power of *The Children's Hour* especially in the throbbing second act. . . . We may view with the same perturbation the fact that the plays written in recent years have so rarely possessed the power that belongs to *The Children's Hour*."[35]

However, *The Children's Hour* has come in for a good deal of criticism. For instance, Lawson actually criticizes Hellman for not writing a social document. He says that "the situation gives the impression of being implausible because it is not placed in a solid social framework. The play ignores time and place. The prejudice against sexual abnormality varies."[36] Besides, we are not shown the conditions in the environment which explain the little girl's demoniac hatred and the suffering of the two school teachers. Furthermore, in later years, it became customary to describe the play as a criticism of the rich and the powerful so much so that Hellman herself had to clarify the import of the play saying: "To my mind the theme of lesbianism is less this time and what comes out stronger is the power of a lie and what it can do to people when it has even one little ounce of truth."[37]

Nevertheless, we may say that *The Children's Hour* is a daring step forward in the theatre's humanizing power to create understanding and empathy for unconscious deviation as a tragic flaw, rather than a loathsome anomaly. Only a playwright as skilfully restrained and impatient with sentimentality as Miss Hellman could have handled such a theme successfully. To exorcize the inexplicable malignancy of the human soul seems Miss

Hellman's special gift.

What is more, *The Children's Hour* is profoundly integrated with its own time. It is to Hellman's credit that she makes the crux of her play not the question of homosexuality itself, but society's savage treatment of the homosexual, arising out of cruelly persisting ignorance. Also, we can see in the play, how an individual conflict may serve to focus attention on its crucial social implications. The play has broken down in thousands of audience their antipathy against its subject and aroused in them the desire for further knowledge. The suicide of Martha raises the important question of the tragic needlessness of her death and of the right of the homosexual to the fullest personal happiness.

Above all, the chief significance of *The Children's Hour* lies in its social statement. The question which remains is whether the gangster or the child is more culpable for the result of such evil than the passive society which permits it to take control. In the final scene of *The Children's Hour*, Hellman defiantly points the finger of guilt at society as a whole. She suggests that adults are too often 'children' while infantile revenge is a matter of course in man's dealings with each other.

Thus, *The Children's Hour* is a striking example of the vital play profoundly integrated with its own time. It is not flawless but the playwright deals with a subject of grave human import in such a way as to carry the theatre forward and to give it its deepest meaning and significance. Great works of art like Aeschylus's *Oresteia*, Shakespeare's *Measure for Measure* and Melville's *Billy Budd* have dealt with the dichotomy between primitive justice and mercy. Although *The Children's Hour* is certainly a less monumental work of art than any of these, it is within its limits, a wholly successful moral play.

NOTES

1. Harry Gilory, "The Bigger the Lie," *Conversations with Lillian Hellman*, ed. Jackson R. Bryer (Jackson: University Press of Mis-

sissippi, 1986), p. 25.

2. Historically speaking lesbianism is hardly revolutionary on the stage. Homosexuality had been portrayed in the Renaissance English drama and it appeared on the modern American stage around 1920. The best known play on lesbianism was *The Captive* (1926), a translation from the French of Edouard Bourdet.
3. Lillian Hellman, "Introduction," *Four Plays* (Random House, 1942), pp. vii-xiv.
4. Barret H. Clark, "Lillian Hellman," *College English*, Vol. 6, No. 3, Dec. 1944, p. 128.
5. Doris V. Falk, *Lillian Hellman* (New York: Frederick & Ungar, 1978), p. 37.
6. Gossip and its handmaiden scandal have been fascinating themes in drama since the seventeenth century when Shakespeare sent Iago in *Othello* about his baleful whispering business to profit of the box office. Sheridan in the eighteenth century with his *The School for Scandal* was followed by Goldoni with his *Women's Gossip*. Echegaray in the nineteenth century with his *El Gram Galeoto* (*The World and His Wife* in the later local adaptation). Lady Gregory in the early twentieth century with her *Spreading the News* and later various other playwrights dealt with the subject.
7. Judith Olauson, *The American Woman Playwright: A View of Criticism and Characterization* (New York: Washington Publishing, 1981), p. 6.
8. Lillian Hellman, *The Children's Hour* in *The Collected Plays* (Boston-Toronto: Little, Brown, 1971), pp. 18-19.
9. Anitha Block, "Contemporary Drama: The Individual in Conflict with Changing Sexual Standards," *The Changing World in Plays and Theatre, 1939* (De Capo Press, 1971), pp. 76-132.
10. Laufe Abe, *Anatomy of a Hit: Long Run Plays on Broadway from 1900 to the Present Day* (New York: Hawthorn, 1966), p. 139.
11. C.W.E. Bigsby, "Lillian Hellman," *A Critical Introduction to Twentieth Century American Drama* (Cambridge University Press, 1982), p. 277.
12. Judith Olauson, *The American Woman Playwright*, p. 6.
13. "The Thunderbolt of Broadway," *Literary Digest*, New York, Vol. 118, No. 22, Dec. 1, 1934, p. 20.
14. Bentley's charge against the plot structure of *The Children's Hour*

invariably reminds us of T.S. Eliot's celebrated remark regarding Shakespeare's *Hamlet* that it is "a film on which two photographs have been taken."

15. Joseph Wood Krutch, "The Heart of a Child," *The Nation*, New York, Vol. CXXXIV, No. 3622, Dec. 5, 1934, pp. 656-57.
16. Laufe Abe, *Anatomy of a Hit*, p. 5.
17. C.W.E. Bigsby, "Lillian Hellman," pp. 277-78.
18. Lillian Hellman, "Introduction," *Four Plays*, pp. vii-xiv.
19. R.C. Reynolds, "Lillian Hellman: The Well-made Melodrama," *Stage Left, The Development of the American Social Drama in the Thirties* (New York: The Whitston, 1986), p. 135.
20. Philip M. Armato, "'Good and Evil' in Lillian Hellman's *The Children's Hour*," *Education Theatre Journal*, Vol. 25, No. 4, Dec. 1973, pp. 443-47.
21. Barret H. Clark, p. 128.
22. George Jean Nathan, "*The Children's Hour*," *Vanity Fair*, Vol. 43, No. 6, February 1935, p. 37.
23. Francis Fergusson, "The Art of Drama in a Changing Perspective," *The Idea of a Theatre, A Study of Ten Plays* (Princeton N.T.: Princeton University Press, 1949), p. 20.
24. Brooks Atkinson, Review of *The Children's Hour*, *New York Times*, November 21, 1934, p. 23.
25. R.C. Reynolds, p. 134.
26. "The Thunderbolt of Broadway," p. 20.
27. C.W.E. Bigsby, "Lillian Hellman," p. 278.
28. Lillian Hellman, "*The Children's Hour*," *Sunday New York Times*, Dec. 14, 1952.
29. Jacob H. Adler, "The Rose and the Fox: Notes on the Southern Drama," *South: Modern Southern Literature in its Cultural Setting* Louis D. Rubin, Jr. and Robert D. Jacobs (Doubleday, 1961), pp. 349-75.
30. Barret H. Clark, p. 128.
31. Lillian Hellman, "Lillian Hellman: An Interview," *Paris Review*, John Philips and Anne Hollander, No. 9, Winter 1965, p. 70.
32. Shakespeare, *The Merchant of Venice*, in *The Complete Works of Shakespeare* (London: Spring Books), p. 203.
33. This theme of the whole community's eagerness to accept the children's stories, though they are shown to be improbable and this same amusity to spread the scandals resulted in McCarthy Witch-

hunt, in which, the same kind of pressure caused people to exaggerate and falsely accuse Hellman before House Committee on un-American Activities.

34. Brooks Atkinson, p. 23.
35. John Gassner, *The Theatre in Our Times* (New York, 1954), p. 406.
36. Lawson, *Theory and Technique of Playwriting* (New York, 1949), pp. 264-66.
37. Lillian Hellman, "New York World," *Telegram and Sun*, Dec. 26, 1952, cited in Katherine Lederer, *Lillian Helman* (Boston: Twayne, 1979), p. 26.

"The Melee of Class Struggle": *Days to Come*

Hellman's second play, *Days to Come* (1936), like *The Children's Hour*, deals with the theme of 'good and evil.' As in *The Children's Hour*, the harm is done not by a 'villain,' but by well-intentioned, self-deluded people. As Hellman herself clearly states, "evil this time, is in the hands of people who don't understand it."[1] The play revolves around the lives of several people involved in a labour strike at a small Ohio factory. Hellman offers two theses in the play—first, the antagonists in the class struggle were moving farther and farther apart, and second, the belief that capitalism needed the support of brutal fascism.

From this it is clear that Hellman, like Sidney Kingsley, moves leftward with *Days to Come*. The play deals with labour strife which results in strike-breaking and presents labour as the moral victor. It is built on the theme of labour unionization like Clifford Odets' *Waiting for Lefty*. Hellman attempts to incorporate various themes regarding the evolving character of labour unions and the conflicts between members of a family. As D.V. Falk observes, *Days to Come* is "a brief foray into the melee of class struggle."[2]

However, as the labour cause is not enough to unify the action, Hellman explores the individual characters who are more often than not confused about their own motives. She presents a family of more or less well-intentioned Americans confronted by the problem of dealing with organised labour when their employees undertake a strike. As Hellman herself puts it, *Days to Come* is "a story of innocent people on both sides who are drawn into conflict and events far beyond their comprehension. It's the saga of a man who started something he cannot stop, a parallel among adults to what I did with children in *The Children's Hour.*"[3]

Though the play is chiefly concerned with labour unionization, it is not conceived in the simple realism of Sklar, Maltz or even Galsworthy, but is interwoven with the complicated, neurotic lives of the industrialists themselves. It is rather an illumination of the forces from which strikes grow than a bare socio-economic photography.

Days to Come is set in a small town in Ohio in which workers are reluctantly striking against their paternalistic employer, Andrew Rodman, who is a part owner of a brush factory, a family business inherited from his father. Hard times have forced Rodman to cut the workers' wages below the poverty level. Some of the less paternalistic stock-holders—Henry Ellicott, the family lawyer, and Rodman's sister, Cora—have persuaded Rodman to break the strike by importing professional strike-breakers, Wilkie, Mossie and Joe, who are mobsters and jailbirds.

The union organizer, Leo Whalen, warns his men not to allow themselves to be provoked by the strike-breakers into rioting or other violence. This results in a long stand-off. One of the strike-breakers, Mossie, is killed by Joe in a gambling quarrel and the gang leader, Wilkie, plants the dead body at Union Headquarters. The workers, and especially Whalen, are made to look guilty of the murder. Whalen is arrested. And a pretext is established for the strike-breakers to attack the workers.

In the ensuing violence, the child of the foreman, Firth, an old friend of Rodman family, is killed. The town is torn apart with shooting. The workers are hungry and tired, and so they agree to call off the strike. Julie Rodman, Andrew's wife, provides an alibi that Whalen is innocent of murder, as she herself was present in his quarters when the corpse was placed near his house by Wilkie. Whalen is released and the workers go back to work. Whalen gives up the attempt to organize a union. Although Andrew Rodman succeeds in breaking the strike, his family life is wrecked. He suffers not only from the social tragedy of this bloodshed, but also from the personal tragedy of his wife's infidelities. At the end, there is a new kind of awareness between Andrew and his wife.

In *Days to Come*, as in *The Searching Wind*, the public and private realms are meant to illustrate each other. The upper-middle class characters mess up their domestic lives with the same disregard for hard reality which they have for social and political questions. Dependent on an ample and secure income, undisturbed by and largely ignorant of the world around them, members of this class exist in unquestioned comfort till the foundations of their economic support are threatened. Then the nullity of their inner lives, the lack of genuine values of mind or spirit grow frighteningly clear, bewildering and oppressive to them, though possibly liberating to a few. They are adrift in an empty universe, provoking a psychological chaos in which, whether they are of good or destructive nature, they must necessarily behave like fools or knaves. They are autonomous of a society which they have never really examined or understood. They barely recognize their own identity. They become a citizenry of the maimed.

Hellman, being an observer and a philosopher, as well as a special pleader, knows well that in the ranks of each of the opposing forces there are those who are neither villains nor heroes. And she has been at pains to show some man or woman who has been victimized, like Andrew Rodman, by the circumstances, is worthy to be saved like Alexandra in *The Little Foxes*.

At the end of the play, Andrew Rodman orders the gangsters out from his house and realizes that it is no longer safe to move out. It is important to note that Andrew is a businessman who is not an exploiter, and that the workers also have a cause. Only the mediators are villainous. The play's message is ambivalent in the sense that while creating a genial industrialist and genuine workers, the blame is shifted on to the mediators. But the questions of the mediators exploiting the situation in itself, as the play suggests, is created by capitalist economy. One cannot break strikes without hurting someone. There is truth in Wilkie's comments:

> But I want to tell you, I've worked for a lot of men, some of the deacons of the Church were breaking strikes for the

> good of America, but I never worked for a man before who believed I could come in, run his factory, and break his strike, without walking on anybody's toes.[4]

The plot construction of *Days to Come* is met with criticism and especially most critics find it faulty in the third act as in the case of *The Children's Hour*. The action of the play starts in the first act, with the strike-breakers entering Rodman's house. The action rises in the second act when one of the trouble creators is killed by his own man. Hellman seems to fall back on a melodramatic intrigue for the climax, allowing the denouement to hinge on an attempt to frame the organizer, Whalen, on a charge of murder. The play reaches the climax when the dead body of Mossie is left at the union leader's house. However, the catastrophe occurs when Rodman's wife, Julie, provides an alibi to release Whalen and confesses to her husband her illicit relationship with Ellicott and Whalen.

The most criticized element of the plot of *Days to Come* is the thread of the wife's love for the labour organizer and the most criticized scene is that in which she confesses her feelings to Whalen. For instance, Barret H. Clark thinks that "the introduction of a love scene at the climax of the action, no matter what it is intended to do, blurs the outline of the story and obscures the theme."[5] Another critic, Katherine Lederer, says that "although Hellman said the play was about individuals, most critics felt that the strike was the story and saw no connection between the strike and the revelation of the personal lives of the characters."[6] There are other critics who find fault with the plot structure as a whole. For example, Harold Clurman writes: "the play's flaw is that its plot does not wholly convey its intended meaning or creative impulse."[7] Bigsby is of the view that "the weakness of the play is that this moral tale is contained within the pieties of a sub-genre—the strike play—which Hellman handled with less assurance . . . she was simultaneously writing two distinct plays. The two proved incompatible."[8] Doris V. Falk feels: "The plot of the play, as a whole, is as abortive as Whalen's efforts. It is crowded with loosely related elements including blackmail, adultery and broadly satirical sketches of the rich."[9] David Sievers says: "the play is strange and jerky in its construction."[10] G.J. Gould, opines: "the play is too complex and poorly structured."[11]

While these various attacks from different critics against the plot construction of *Days to Come* as abortive, jerky and poorly structured, cannot be dismissed as baseless, it is to be remembered that this is due to the very nature of the play itself. Though *The Children's Hour* deals with the same theme of the war between forces of good and evil, its plot is tightly constructed because of the factor that evil clearly emerges as the victor. But inasmuch as *Days to Come* is about evil 'in the hands of those who don't understand it' and since, in Hellman's scheme, ignorance is no excuse, a play based on this proposition is bound to be comparatively discursive and undramatic. As a passage in *The Bible* read:

> For there is no remembrance of the wise more than of the fool for ever: seeing that which is in the days to come shall all be forgotten. And how dieth the wise man? As the fool. ('Ecclesiastes' 2:16)

The title of the play, derived from this quotation, indicates that the forces of good have no direction except muddle and neglect. And the only reward of such failure is a dim self-insight when it is too late to reform.

It is also to be noted that while such things as infidelity are "always happening in life and spoiling the pattern which tidy-minded artists must weave to make themselves articulate, they are too likely to lead us into bypaths, away from the main issue."[12] It is, perhaps, for this reason and also because of Hellman's desire to find 'new ways to say' what she has to say that she feels impelled to pull together the threads of her arguments in the last scene resulting in chaotic construction.

The point is that in constructing the play, Hellman draws obviously more on her own feelings as a moralist than on her artistic obligations as a dramatic artist. She seemed to be aware of this artistic immaturity at this stage of her dramatic career. This is made clear to us in her memoirs when she says: "I am a learner, not a teacher and I need a cool teacher."[13] This is driven home to us further by her own response to the criticism levelled against the poorly constructed plot of *Days to Come* in her Introduction to *Four Plays.* Hellman says how she had made the conventional mistake of trying to pack everything she knew into the play:

> I returned to the amateur's mistake. Everything you think and feel must be written this time, because you may never have another chance to write it. . . . I wanted to say too much. And I began thinking of new ways to say it. People in life, I told myself, don't always make the direct answer, or follow the immediately preceding thought. . . . I played this theme all alone. A solitary composer with a not very interesting quarter note. The subtleties of failures are seldom discovered and that is just as well.[14]

Like the plot-construction, Hellman's art of characterization, in *Days to Come*, has come in for a good deal of criticism. It is generally believed that the play lacks focus and depth of characterization. The characters, though vigorously committed to their beliefs, seem to be bound by the playwright's harness rather than their own.

Here, it is important to note that the characters in *Days to Come* are different people, in quite different situations. As the play is about a strike in a 'model' town, its characters are a confused array of employers—Andrew Rodman and Henry Willicott, of idle neurotic women—Julie Rodman and Cora Rodman, of strike leaders—Whalen, of workers—Firth, of strike-breakers—Wilkie, Mossie and Joe. What is more, the characters stand by and allow the despoilers to accomplish their destructive aims. Often these bystanders may be the victims of their own naivete or lack of self-knowledge. Hellman has placed her characters in a nightmarish situation, a refining fire, to test their integrity.

Andrew Rodman is a kind and decent factory owner in a

town where he has known most of his workers and their families all his life. In him, we have a portrait of a naively docile workman and a knowing and effective labour leader. He is an idealist who is on the verge of bankruptcy because he plays a good Samaritan to his wife's family. He has many virtues—love for his men, love for his wife, love for his town and love for his business. He, therefore, pays for loving all of them neither wisely nor well. Rodman sounds like a gentleman farmer when he speaks of his love for his town and for his men,.but the gentleman farmer never understood the peasant any more than the industrialist on the hill understood the workers in the valley.

Rodman clings to the liberal virtues, but does so in an abstract way, protected by his money from the harsh casualties of life. As he belatedly realises, he has been "the delicate prince in his ivory tower, carefully protected from the dust and din of battle."[15] His liberal vacillation has been the cause of the collapse of the world he fondly imagines himself to inhabit. As a benevolent manufacturer and reluctant oppressor, Rodman turns out to be a well-meaning but unbelievably naive cuckold. As a humanitarian businessman who might have ingratiated himself, he is caught between a venal partner and an unfaithful wife. All the same, he is so broken up over the death of a striker's child that his wife's infidelity is only secondary to him.

Thus, Andrew Rodman comes to us as a victim of the brutalities of the system which he hopes to humanise. He is a spoiled priest who believes that the world could be sustained by his own moral imagination, and he could play the game of wealth without being corrupted, and that his wife's desperate sense of alienation could be controlled by his own sense of moral purpose. In the words of Bigsby, "the inadequacy of such a stance, the incubus of anarchy concealed beneath apparent order, is symbolized here, as in Fitzgerald's book, by the wife's adultery. And he is left at the end of the play discarded by history, and displaced from the comfortable world he had imagined himself to inhabit, like Fitzgerald's Dick Diver."[16]

Julie, Andrew Rodman's wife, is an interesting character. She contracts a loveless marriage and drifts aimlessly, indulging in extramarital affairs because she inhabits a world with no values of any kind. Being a member of the ruling class and bored by the dull town and loveless marriage, Julie becomes wilfully unfaithful with a variety of men. She has an affair with Andrew's business partner, Henry Ellicott. She meets the Union leader, Whalen, and falls in love with him also. With her insatiable drive and her restless seeking for sensation, she seems to be "Hedda Gabler without even the compassion that Ibsen evokes for his neurotic heroine."[17]

However, Julie Rodman need not be dismissed wholly as an unfaithful wife. She is not the bored aristocrat, slumming with a labour organizer, because she is a closet socialist. She believes that there are people who learn from others and that she is a constant learner. This is made clear when she says to Whalen:

> When I was young, I guess I was looking for something I could do. Then for something I could be. Finally, just for something to want, or to think or to believe in. I always wanted somebody to show me the way. . . . I decided long time ago that there were people who had to learn from other people. I'm one of them. (111)

We may say that it is with these two characters—Andrew and Julie Rodman—that the play rises momentarily above the conventionalities of the strike drama. Their failure in their lives is not a sudden failure of will and imagination. Hellman's point is that it is a self-deceit of long standing which has merely been exposed by the brutal realities of the 1930s. "Neither Andrew nor his wife has been in touch with the real world at any time in their lives. Born to wealth, they have been disabled by the presumptions of power, but also by the empty posturings of a decade in which morality was conceived as a private testing of the sensibility or that pursuit of the ineffable ideal, with its underside of self-deceiving or corrupting violence, which Fitzgerald had described in *The Great Gatsby*."[18]

Cora, Andrew's sister, falls a total contrast to him. In the figure of Cora, Hellman offers a version of Regina in *The Little*

Foxes and a reprise of the self-concerned aunt in *The Children's Hour*, her first play. Cora is a woman for whom self is the central and motivating force. She is unmarried and the co-owner of the factory and is portrayed as a frustrated spinster and as a caricature of the snobbish, greedy, idle rich. She is a pathetic, psychosomatic woman who acts like a child fussing with the servants, hating her brother's wife with an incestuous jealousy and knowing so little of sex that she thinks Caesarian operations are when the woman is under age. Hellman says in her Introduction to *Four Plays* that she 'hates a woman like Cora.'

Whalen, the labour organizer, is the first of the few Hellman 'heroes.' He is one of the characters who compels Hellman's respect as a man 'who works for other men.' He is an intelligent and courageous union leader. As Timothy J. Wiles notices, "Hellman places the vision in the eyes of Whalen's character, looking to it in the future."[19] The faithful worker Firth reminds us of the feudal loyalty of Chekhov's Firs: He is a noble workman whose child is killed by the vicious strike-breakers.

Among the vicious characters, Henry Ellicott Wilkie, Mossie and Joe, Henry Ellicott is the corrupt and scheming lawyer, the single-mindedly grasping capitalist shareholder of the factory. He is Julie's ex-lover and the foxiest of little foxes. And Wilkie, Mossie and Joe are strike-breakers who are imported by the manipulation of Ellicott to create violence in Ohio. They are atypical thugs and they are restless because they are not able to make a massacre for which they have been trained. Their restlessness creates an unhealthy tension that leads one of them to kill Mossie.

All these characters, good or bad, however ingeniously sketched, are ineffectual. And their efforts, along with the plot, just peter out. The hired thugs—Wilkie and Joe—accomplish the villainous purpose for which they are finally paid and leave town. The strike as well as the unionization fail, the company would probably go broke and the marriage of the well-meaning Rodman is bankrupt. Julie's adulterous affair with Ellicott has gone sour, and her mawkish attraction to Whalen comes to nothing. For Julie, it is too late, and her impulse to find a better way of life has been too long delayed. Nothing can be expected from Henry Ellicott who brings in the strike-breakers. Obviously he is only a stupid, unimaginative and well-intentioned bungler. And, as for Cora, she remains a lay figure, the symbol of all that was blind and cruel among the economic royalists who produced her. The workers have gone back to their tedious, under-paid jobs, and the Rodmans go back to their strenuous, trapped, unsatisfying lives.

In spite of its lapses in plot-construction and characterization, *Days to Come*, like any other play of Hellman, holds up a mirror to the contemporary issues and is always praised for its realistic nature. The play is a result of Hellman's sincere effort to dramatise immediate social forces. The script is of interest to the student of Hellman's work because of her attempt to enlarge the boundaries of the realistic play. "She gathered information from newspapers, special reports, political discussions, meetings that were prevalent at the time."[20]

In contrast to *The Children's Hour*, *Days to Come* has obvious contemporary meaning. As the play reveals, it is naive to imagine that one can break a strike without violence. Also, the discussion about the domestic difficulties that mirror the social problems trivialises them. As Bigsby observes, "certainly Lillian Hellman's moral concerns are obscured by a more immediate social imperative, while its characters stand as a simple concession to the conventionalities of the committed theatre."[21] Hellman herself confesses this social implication in her play:

> It is crowded and overwrought, but it is a good report of rich liberals in 1930s, of a labour leader who saw through them, of a modern lost lady, and has in it a correct prediction of how conservative the American labour movement was to become.[22]

Moreover, the characters in the play are based on real people. This is made clear to us by Hellman herself in her Introduction to *Four Plays*:

> I knew a woman like Cora and I hated her, and that hate had to go in the play. I knew a woman like Julie, I pitied her, and that pity had to go in the play. I had been raised with the Ellicotts of the world and what I felt about them had to go in the play, too. I knew Leo Whalen and I wanted to say how much I respected men who work for other men.[23]

Although in *Days to Come* irony is sparingly used when compared to the rest of her plays, still one can see the 'boomerang irony' in the plot. In emphasizing the fact that ignorance, dishonesty and cowardice in personal lives affect social events, Hellman makes use of 'boomerang irony.' If the factory owner and his wife had understood their own motives, had been honest in their marriage, then he would not have been in the financial clutches of the lawyer and would not have been forced to call in the strike-breakers. If the owner's sister had not been selfish and greedy, Rodman could have used money instead of borrowing from the lawyer. Thus, the mistakes of the main characters turn out on them.

One should not fail to note that Hellman, in *Days to Come*, is attempting a technique which she later mastered in *The Autumn Garden* and *Toys in the Attic*, attempting to show more sides of a character than the drama normally reveals. Several reviewers called the play novelistic. Hellman has always insisted that "she has been influenced by novelists, such as Henry James, Stendhal and Dickens, rather than by dramatists."[24]

Hellman is charged of writing in *Days to Come* a melodrama including murder, attempted frame-up, coincidence, attempted blackmail and secrets. Falk writes: "*Days to Come*, however, took Hellman's characteristic form—realistic melodrama."[25] Leonard Ungar says: "unable to write tragedy and unwilling to settle for melodrama, she writes both: a tragedy in a melodramatic setting where an individual brings ruin on himself and others because he does not understand the nature of man."[26]

But, one should understand that these are the melodramatic trappings typical of too many plays of the 1930s. They are not false. All this is only representative of what was or had been happening in the earlier days of the period.

In *The Searching Wind, The Autumn Garden* and *Toys in the Attic*, Hellman looks at the Rodmans of the world—the ineffectual ones who let evil and decay attack and destroy the lives of others, as it consumes their own vitality. Though flawed and tantalizing in the sketchy glimpses of the Rodmans it gives us, *Days to Come* is an interesting play. Drama critic, John Gassner, looking back at the 1940s, feels that "*Days to Come* deserves better of New York than the fate it received."[27] Joseph Wood Krutch and Alexander Taylor were among the few who praised Hellman's attempt to expand her dramatic canvas. Also, Krutch recognized the Hellman of *Days to Come* "as an heir to the playwright August Strindberg."[28]

Days to Come illustrates the fusion of socio-economic themes with psychoanalytic treatment of motives in this post-Freudian period. Hellman, a better playwright than propagandist, seems more intent on probing the psyches and souls of stupid capitalists than on preaching the thesis or on summoning the workers to revolution.

The main significance of *Days to Come* lies in its largest defect. As Clurman puts it, "Hellman has certainly written better plays than *Days to Come* yet I found it interesting for a variety of reasons even for its faults. The play takes on a measure of dignity a promise that greater technical assurance through further practice will give Hellman, her individual tone."[29] Although Hellman lacked the knowledge and social awareness required to write a protest drama, of the working class pitted against its decadent and corrupt oppressors, the play does, especially in the last act, begin to indicate her understanding of the personal conflicts of the middle class family.

However confused and diffuse the total effect, *Days to Come* has many qualities of Hellman's plays. Shifting tensions permeate the atmosphere. We sense the unresolved discords, the sultry hates and murderous impulses that lie below the surface. The utterances may often be quiet and decorous, yet there is a burning intensity behind them. From the anger and hatred she exhibited in *The Children's Hour* against the Tilfords and the furious, underlying evil she shows to be present in the Rodman family in *Days to Come*, she is moulding another attempt to bring the form of social drama to bear on the plight of the middle class.

Indeed, *Days to Come* is a play best seen in the context of a book like *Tender is the Night* rather than in that provided by the strike plays blossoming in the American theatre of the time. However, it is interesting to conclude with Hellman's words on the play:

> But with all that is wrong, all the confusion, the jumble, the attempt to do too much, I stand on the side of *Days to Come*. I am only sorry that the confusion in the script confused the best director in the theatre.[30]

NOTES

1. Lillian Hellman, Introduction to *Four Plays* (Randon House, 1942), p. ii.
2. Doris. V. Falk, *Lillian Hellman* (New York: Frederick Ungar, 1978), p. 45.
3. Lillian Hellman, *Herald Tribune*, December 13, 1936.
4. Lillian Hellman, *Days to Come* in *The Collected Plays* (Boston: Little, Brown, 1971), p. 128.
5. Barret H. Clark, "Lillian Hellman," *College English*, Vol. 6, No. 3 Dec. 1944, p. 130.
6. Katherine Lederer, *Lillian Hellman* (Boston: Twayne, 1979), pp. 34-35.
7. Harold Clurman, "Theatre: *Days to Come*," *The Nation*, Vol. 227. No. 18, November 25, 1978, pp. 586-88.
8. C.W.E. Bigsby, "Lillian Hellman," *A Critical Introduction to Twentieth Century American Drama* (Cambridge University Press, 1982), p. 279.
9. D.V. Falk, *Lillian Hellman*, p. 48.
10. David Sievers, "Freudian Fraternity of the Thirties," *Freud on Broadway* (New York: Hermitage House, 1955), p. 281.

11. G.J. Gould, "Lillian Hellman," *Modern American Playwrights* (New York: Dodd, Mead, 1966), p. 174.
12. Barret. H. Clark, "Lillian Hellman," *College English*, p. 130.
13. Lillian Hellman, *Pentimento: A Book of Portraits* (Boston: Little, Brown, 1973), p. 160.
14. Lillian Hellman, "An Introduction to *Four Plays*," "The Playwright," *The Passionate Playgoer*, ed. George Oppenheimer (New York: The Viking Press, 1958), pp. 296-97.
15. C.W.E. Bigsby, p. 278.
16. *Ibid.*, pp. 278-79.
17. David Sievers, p. 281.
18. C.W.E. Bigsby, p. 278.
19. Timothy J. Wiles, "Lillian Hellman's American Political Theatre: The Thirties and Beyond," Mark W. Estrin, ed., *Critical Essays on Lillian Hellman* (Boston, Mass: G.K. Hall, 1989), p. 94.
20. Harold Clurman, "Theatre: *Days to Come*," pp. 586-88.
21. C.W.E. Bigsby, p. 277.
22. Lillian Hellman, *Pentimento: A Book of Portraits*, p. 163.
23. Lillian Hellman, Introduction to *Four Plays,* p. 11.
24. "Lillian Hellman, Interview" cited in Katherine Lederer, p. 35.
25. Doris V. Falk, *Lillian Hellman*, p. 46.
26. Leonard Ungar, *American Writers*, Supplement I, Part I (New York: Charles Scribner, 1964), p. 278.
27. John Gassner, cited in Katherine Lederer, p. 37.
28. Joseph Wood Krutch, cited in Mark W. Estrin, p. 11.
29. Harold Clurman, pp. 586-88.
30. Lillian Hellman, "The Playwright," *The Passionate Playgoer*, p. 297.

Social Degradation and Moral Decay: *The Little Foxes*

Take us the foxes, the little foxes that spoil the
Vines; for our vines have tender grapes.

Song of Solomon, II, 15

Generally regarded as Hellman's best play, *The Little Foxes* (1938) is most tense and biting drama. Like Ben Jonson's *Volpone* and *The Alchemist*, it is based on human greed and rapacity. Taken from 'Song of Solomon' in the *Bible*, the title refers to greedy and avaricious human beings who spoil the vineyards of the world to get the grapes of their desire. Hellman's little foxes are rapacious and are wolves that eat their own kind.

Hellman was stimulated by the social upheaval of the 1930s in writing *The Little Foxes*. It offers a scathing criticism of a class of people who manipulate society and the lives within it with a ruthless eye toward greater personal wealth and power. The play implicitly condemns the vindictiveness and rapacity of bourgeois society. It is a sombre study in the psychology of evil. Thus, *The Little Foxes* is concerned with social degradation and moral decay as inescapable consequences of the inordinate appetite for money and power.

As the title suggests, *The Little Foxes* is a gripping story of the Hubbards, who, like the little foxes, are noted for their greed and covetousness. The Hubbards are, indeed, a menace to the vineyards of the world, preying upon society and tearing at each other. The parable is directed towards those who watch the little foxes at their work but who build no fences and set traps too late to ensnare them. Undoubtedly, in the playwright's mind, as the play took shape was the underlying idea that the actions of the Hubbards exemplified the inhumanity and vices of capitalism.

Set in the home of Regina and Horace Giddens, in a small Southern town in 1900, *The Little Foxes* concerns itself with the conflicts which grow out of a business deal between a Chicago industrialist, Marshall, and Ben and Oscar Hubbard and their sister Regina Giddens. It would be difficult to find a more malignant gang of petty robber barons than Miss Hellman's chief characters. Hellman did her home work on the rise of the Southern industry, which was beginning at that time to compete with the industry of New England. The industrial revolution is the backdrop against which the 'foxes' play their human or inhuman roles.

The two brothers, Ben Hubbard and Oscar Hubbard, have inherited their father's wealth and are anxious to build a cotton factory along with Regina Giddens in partnership with Mr. Marshall, a Chicago businessman. Marshall has put up forty-nine per cent of the money, and the three Hubbards will put the remaining fifty one per cent. Regina's, of course, will come out from her banker husband, Horace. This is revealed to us in their conversation:

Regina: (slowly) And what does that mean?
(Ben shrugs, looks towards Oscar)

Oscar: (Looks at Ben, clears throat) Well, Regina, it's like this. For forty-nine percent Marshall will put up four hundred thousand dollars. For fifty one percent (smiles archly) a controlling interest, mind you, we will put up two hundred and twenty five thousand dollars besides offering him certain benefits that our (looks to Ben) local position allows us to manage. Ben means that two hundred and twenty thousand dollars is lot of money.

Regina: I know the terms and I know it's a lot of money.

Ben: (Nodding) It is.

Oscar: Ben means that we are ready with our two thirds of the money. Your third, Horace's I mean, doesn't seem to be ready. (Raises his hand as Regina starts to speak) Ben has written to Horace, I have written and you have written the answers. But he never mentions this business.[1]

But Horace, who is being treated for a heart ailment in the hospital at John Hopkins, has not come up with his share of money. The brothers threaten to cut Regina out and find another partner if the money is not forthcoming. But Regina knows that they do not want to take in a stranger. When the brothers put pressure on Regina, she sends her daughter, Alexandra, to Baltimore to bring Horace home. She bargains with the brothers for a larger share. She and Ben agree that it will come from Oscar's share. When Oscar objects, they suggest to him that Alexandra may marry his son Leo. Birdie, Oscar's aristocrat wife, whom Oscar married for the cotton and the land, over-hears this conversation. Thus, in the first act, Hellman draws a picture of greed and corruption among middle class characters whose only thoughts are of profit and personal gain.

The second conflict in the play occurs when Regina, worried about Horace's continued silence regarding the business deal, sends Alexandra to bring him home in spite of his illness. Horace comes home and is informed about the Hubbard machinations by the faithful servant Addie. Horace refuses to give Regina the money. Now close to death, Horace has no interest in joining Regina and her brothers in exploiting the town's cheap labour force. He rails at her:

> I'm sick of you, sick of this house, sick of my life here, I'm sick of your brothers and their dirty tricks to make a dime. Why should I give you the money? To pound the bones of this town to make dividends for you to spend? You wreck the town, you and your brothers. (183)

With Leo's help, the brothers steal bonds worth $ 88,000 from Horace's safe-deposit box, bonds which are negotiable as money, and Oscar takes them to Chicago to make up the missing third share of the investment.

And, when Horace learns that the two brothers have stolen money from his safe-deposit box to finance his share of the deal, he strikes back through Regina, telling her that he will disinherit her, leaving all to Alexandra so that she can escape the town, the family and especially a forced marriage with Leo. Horace prevents Regina's getting the upper hand by telling her he will say that he lent the bonds to the Hubbard brothers. Regina will get only the bonds in his will. Regina is trapped. She will receive nothing from her brothers except as they choose. But the next move is hers. Regina challenges:

> But I won't let you punish me. If you won't do anything I will now. (She starts for the door) (194)

In the course of their quarrel, she and Horace go over their past. She tells Horace that she has always had only contempt for him:

> I told you I married you for something. It turned out it was only for this. (carefully) This wasn't what I wanted, but it was something. I never thought about it much, but if I had (Horace puts his hand to his throat) I'd have known that you would die before I would. But I couldn't have known that you would get heart trouble so early and so bad. I'm lucky, Horace, I've always been lucky. I'll be lucky again. (195)

Thus, Regina manages to defeat Horace in the end. When Horace asks her to call the maid, Addie, to get the medicine bottle from upstairs, Regina, without moving an inch and even without blinking her eye, stares at him. He calls Addie in panic, then tries to climb the stairs, and collapses. When she is sure that he is unconscious, she calls the servants. Thus Horace's conversion to good comes too late to save either his town or his daughter. Regina has triumphed as a force of evil, and whatever intentions Horace had, to thwart her and her brothers' plans, die along with him.

The brothers arrive. Leo tells them that Horace knows about the theft. Regina tells them that she knows about it also. She confronts her brothers with the theft and threatens to send them to jail, unless she gets the lion's share of the new business. Now she has the upper hand. She says:

> I'm smiling Ben, I'm smiling because you're quite safe while Horace lives. . . . I shall want seventy five percent in exchange for the bonds. . . . And if I don't get what I want, I am going to put all three of you in jail. (201)

She apparently wins, but at the end of the play Alexandra asks her mother: "What was Papa doing on the staircase?" (203) The implications of her questions are not lost on Ben who threatens to use them eventually against her sister. But Regina is still the queen. Alexandra refuses to stay with her, to watch the foxes 'eat the earth.' The only suggestion of vulnerability in Regina now is her invitation to Alexandra to sleep in the same room with her. To this her daughter replies: "Are you afraid Mama?" (207)

While the optimism expressed in Alexandra's final rejection climaxes the final conflict in the play—the conflict between Alexandra and a future champion of evil—it is cautiously tempered. The point of the play, therefore, is that the battle between those who are evil is possibly more significant than the possibility of the triumph of good over them. Neither Horace nor Alexandra is victorious as a force of good, for his struggle has killed him and she lacks a full understanding of how ruthless the forces of evil can be.

The Little Foxes is known for its best plot construction. Hellman carefully structures the action in a close-knit progression of events. Crescendos of violence are prepared for and built toward as the suspense rises within each act and in the play as a whole. The action is a series of power struggles from which Regina's daughter, Alexandra, will finally escape.

The plot of *The Little Foxes* consists of "a series of crises, each one partly resolved so that the audience is kept waiting for the resolution to be completed, only to be surprised or shocked by a reversal leading to a new crisis."[2] The climax is reached in the quarrel and the death of Horace.

The entire first act is an outstanding example of dramatic exposition. The revelation of the past weaves naturally and unobtrusively through the opening dialogue. From the moment of Birdie's breathless, overgay entrance and Oscar's sadistic smashing of her pleasure, the strains of personal antagonism become immediately clear. In front of their guest, the vicious clan display their ignorance, their hypocrisy and their greed, while Marshall, the outsider, serves as a catalyst to bring out details which the audience must know.

The remaining two acts maintain this well-built structure as each scene further intensifies what has already been adroitly established. There is not a single loose end throughout the entire play to distract or mislead at any point. Hellman has made her drama air-tight.

Although the structure of *The Little Foxes* is unanimously praised, some critics feel that the ending of the play is ambiguous. For instance, Richard Lockridge, reviewing the 1939 production of *The Little Foxes*, says that "toward the end the movement falters and the pivotal character [Regina] goes slightly out of focus."[3] What the critics seem to have missed to note is that Hellman has consciously made the ending ambiguous. It is clearly an example of her 'open-ended technique.' Hellman deliberately ends her plays on an intermediate note with a view to leaving the audience to wonder as to what the characters do with their lives. As Smiley rightly observes, "the play remains unfinished, because Hellman's mode does not move completely into art which interprets life, but remains art which imitates life, translated through the 'drama as weapon' mood of the thirties."[4]

The ingenuity of plot construction of *The Little Foxes* is happily matched with Hellman's superb art of characterization. Her characters talk and move in a believably realistic fashion without seeming to be arbitrarily led through mechanical paces for the mere creation of an effect. The concentrated evil of her central characters and the lack of any saving grace of human compassion make the sordidness virtually unrelieved.

The characters of *The Little Foxes* are conceived as a natural part of society in which they live and remain unattractive and repugnant as human beings, fascinating in their horror as 'snarling beasts.' Moreover, the Hubbards are in complete control of their destinies. Outside influences work on them with great strength, but there is no evidence of any compulsion or raw force of nature that has placed them where they are contrary to their own desires. Nothing around them in their physical or social world compels them to act as they do. As opportunists, vicious and without conscience, they proceed entirely on their own, make their own decisions, and have no one but themselves to whom they must render account. The drama of their ugly lives is believably real. Hellman sees the Hubbards as funny in their role-playing and scheming but dangerous.

The individual characters in *The Little Foxes* uniformly maintain their convincing identities as dramatic creations because their baseness has emerged from plausible reality and is explained in a logical fashion.

Regina is the most prominent character in the play. As the curtain goes up, Hellman describes Regina as a handsome, self-assured lady who, along with her brothers Ben and Oscar, takes part in the business deal with Mr. Marshall, a Chicago capitalist. She knows what she wants and is determined to get it, at any cost. When Horace discovers that the bonds were stolen by her brothers and tells her that he is not going to take any action on them, thereby rendering her powerless, she does not lose her courage and will-power. In turn, she allows her husband to die, without giving him the necessary medicine. She confronts her brothers with the theft of the bonds and threatens to send them to jail unless she gets the lion's share. She regains her power over her brothers and rules over them like a queen.

Though Regina does not love her husband, she is clever enough to fight his battles for him in his absence, for her selfish interest. Like Tennessee Williams's Magi, the cat, Regina, the little fox, fights her own battle. Although Regina does not have any love for Horace, circumstances forced her to marry Horace, a small town clerk. But, being a cunning little fox, Regina tries to get money and power through Horace.

Regina is too selfish a mother to take interest in her daughter's welfare. In her pursuit of money and power, she loses her daughter Alexandra's love. Alexandra loves her aunt Birdie more than her mother. But at the end, when Alexandra sees her family as they are, her mother and uncles, she wants to get away from this den, as she knows that her father would want her to go. Thus, Regina stands alone, isolated and alienated even from her daughter.

Small wonder, therefore, if Regina has been considered a villain, and a 'monstrous creature' and one of the most formidable women characters in the history of American drama by some critics. For instance Katherine Lederer says: "Before woman's liberation, Regina would have been considered masculine, if anything she is like Lady Macbeth, unsexed."[5] Other critics like Allen Lewis have dismissed Regina as "a scheming woman, or as the vixen of the den deprived of the understandable human qualities of her sex."[6]

But a close study of the play reveals that Regina is a woman in every physical sense, a beautiful, gracious and dignified hostess, and one who seeks the things a woman is expected to desire—elegance, social position, public respect. Regina is portrayed in three different roles—as sister, wife and mother. As Regina means 'Queen,' whatever role she assumes, she makes sure that victory is hers. And to achieve her goal, she does not mind playing whatever role she wants.

Regina's character can be properly understood and appreciated once we look at her from the feminist angle. Interestingly enough, Hellman herself has done so while portraying Regina. Although she exposes the wrongdoings of her protagonist, she also wants her audience to comprehend what motivated the unscrupulous behaviour of this character. After *The Little Foxes* was produced, Hellman insisted that she had not conceived of Regina as a villain. Hellman might have disapproved of Regina, but she did not dislike her. Hellman observed on another occasion: "I think Regina's kind of funny. If anything, I was amused with her."[7]

What amused Hellman was Regina's cleverness and tenacity, her ability to hold her own with her scheming brothers who are determined to keep her helpless and dependant. Like Ibsen's Hedda Gabler, Regina is frustrated by her lack of power and autonomy. Despite being her father's favourite, she is cheated of her inheritance when he leaves his money to her brothers. After she has helped to hasten her husband's death, she says to Ben: "Ah! Ben, if papa had only left me his money." (205)

Hellman's generation wrote for a populist theatre where feminism was not yet common currency though the issue is clearly at stake in her own work. The figure of Regina Giddens both demonstrates and exploits the familiar politics of repression—racial, economic and sexual. Little foxes, like Regina, do not come from nowhere. Though Regina is clearly as rapacious as her brothers—Ben and Oscar—the methods she is forced to employ reveal the limitations imposed by the 'secondness' of her sexuality. Hellman's woman rises above these unacceptable conditions, but she does so by achieving no new consciousness and no new sense of her world. The grapes are there to be seized, not shared. A daughter rather than a son, Regina has no access to the power that money, which passed on from father to son, provides. The patriarchal society in which she is raised in effect disinherits her and consequently she must depend on the largesse of her brothers or her husband. In 1968, Hellman said: "Money has been the subject of a great deal of literature because it . . . isn't only money of course, it's power, it's sex, it's great many other things."[8]

So, without any money of her own, Regina cannot hope to escape from the stifling small town in Alabama where she was born and go to live in Chicago. Although she longs to begin her life again in the more sophisticated city of Chicago, it seems as distant to her as the 'Moscow' for which Chekhov's provincial three sisters constantly yearn. Thus Regina becomes one of the primal spoilers, a Southern, white male patriarchal figure in drag. Though Hellman ultimately does not sanction the lengths to which Regina is willing to go to acquire money and power, she nevertheless enables us to comprehend what motivates this frustrated woman whose aspirations have been thwarted at every turn. Goldstein observes: "seldom has the evil of materialism received such detailed characterization as in Miss Hellman's protagonist."[9] The impulse behind Regina's power hunger is precisely her own belief in the mediocrity of her social position. Rather than a victim of her society, like Karen and Martha of *The Children's Hour*, Regina is its product.

The next most important character in the play is Ben Hubbard, the eldest of the 'foxes,' who is very intelligent, cunning and rapacious. He tells Regina about South industrialization: "The world is open. Open for people like you and me. Ready for us. Waiting for us. After all, this is just the beginning." (204) Hellman describes Ben as "rather Jolly and far less solemn than the others and far more dangerous."[10] Full of false joviality and platitudes which mask the shrewdness with which he operates, Ben blandly tells Zan good bye before her trip to bring Horace home from Baltimore: "Have a nice trip, Alexandra. The food on the train is very good. The celery is so crisp. Have a good time and act like a little lady." (158)

Regina's decision to get Horace home is instigated by Ben himself with a bitter argument about her share. The gentility with which he coaxes Alexandra is all hypocritical gentility. Ben, like Lophakin in Chekhov's play, *The Cherry Orchard*, displaces the aristocrats from their home, as he announces that he had brought 'Lionnet,' the family plantation, and taken over 'their land, their cotton and their daughter.' It is he who invented that scheme and also manipulates Leo to steal his uncle's bonds while arranging to extricate himself from any blame in the affair. Also, the plan of arranging marriage between Leo and Alexandra is Ben's malice for the sake of money. In another quick plot turn, when Alexandra implies that she is suspicious about her father's death, Ben says with a smile: "Alexandra, you're turning out to be a quite interesting girl." (205) Ben and Regina find each other amusing, even when one is being outwitted by the other.

The other two Hubbards—Oscar and his son Leo—are both weak-willed persons. They lack individuality and are dictated by the elder brother, Ben. Oscar often has to interpret Ben to the not-too-quick-witted Leo. In turn, Ben interprets their sister, Regina, to Oscar. With their lust for power and money, they, along with Ben, descend to perjury, theft and even to wild threat of murder accusation to dislodge Regina from power and money.

Hellman differentiates the villains from each other. Marshall knows that the Hubbards will make profits by paying low wages to unorganized workers and is honest about his motives. Leo, who beats horses, is naive and more slow-witted than his father Oscar, who beats his wife. Oscar is less intelligent than Ben—who spouts high-sounding motives, lets others act illegally and protects himself by refusing to hear details—and then Regina differs from Oscar and Leo in more than intelligence. They bend Oscar to their wills, are composed during emergencies, and appreciate each other's manoeuvrings. As in Shakespeare's *Richard II*, and Ben Jonson's *Volpone*, the villains—Ben, Oscar, Leo and Regina—have their own callous charm.

Pitted against these cunning Hubbards in the play are the people who allow them to rise—Birdie, Horace, Addie and Alexandra. Birdie, the faded aristocratic sister-in-law of the heroine, Regina, is described as "a woman approaching forty, with a pretty well-bred, faded face. Her movements are usually nervous and timid." (152) Birdie is a total contrast to Hubbards in general and Regina in particular. Caught in the den of the foxes—Ben, Oscar and Regina—is the poor lamb, Birdie. Oscar married Birdie because of her social standing and property. Birdie who has great similarity to both Laura and Blanche of Tennessee Williams, is a gentle, weak, ineffectual relic of the old plantation. She is a submissive wife whom Oscar married in order to acquire the family plantation, Lionnet. It is clear in the play that Oscar is the Lord and Master of Birdie who possesses not only her body but also her mind. Birdie, as her name itself suggests, is totally "ineffective, a fluttering bird like creature, wholly cowed by her husband."[11] In the words of O'Hara:

> Birdie is an echo of the old South of plantation aristocracy and noblesse oblige; she moves through the new ways like a remembered refrain which recalls the dignity and grace and pride of less hurried days but loses its identity among the strident notes of uncompassionate new industries and insatiable new greeds, Birdie knows her place among these Hubbards. When she married Oscar, she literally married

> into the family different from her own with its stately seat at Lionnet.[12]

Birdie, who is desperately frustrated, tries to live in the past clinging to the memories of a gentle, lovely mother and brave, kind, soldier father at the old plantation. Her cherished memories of the past sustain her to endure her present life amidst the Hubbards. Birdie looks down in humiliation on hearing herself described as a chattel who is owned by the Hubbards along with the cotton plantation. Birdie always persuades her husband Oscar, to stop shooting: "I want you to stop shooting, I mean, so much. I don't like to see animals and birds killed just for the killing. You only throw them away." (151) Birdie's sensitive mind is hurt by this brutal act of Oscar. Cruelly indifferent to her, Oscar finds an outlet for his sadism by going hunting every morning, having only missed one day in eight years. The delicate sensitive bird like Birdie is also a poor prey caught by the cruel hunter Oscar.

And in this forest of little foxes, the only shelter for Birdie is the warmth and love of Alexandra—daughter of Regina and Horace Giddens. In Alexandra or Zan, she finds a kindred spirit. Suppressed and dominated by the Hubbards, yearning for love and affection in this wood of darkness, Birdie loves Alexandra more than her son Leo. She says: "But you are more to me—more to me than my own child. I love you more than anybody else." (159) Again this intense love for Alexandra prompts her to give a warning to Zan to escape from the den of foxes. Though she submits meekly to her bondage, she wants Alexandra to cut the fetters and soar high. For this she risks the wrath of Oscar. On another occasion she scolds Zan not to love her more: "Because in twenty years you'll just be like me. They'll do all the same things to you." (189) With this prophecy, Birdie leaves the stage.

The only time Birdie is happy is when she is in the pleasant company of Horace and Alexandra. As Falk observes, "Birdie is the pathetic victim, she may be weak-willed, but she is also sensitive and musical, with longing for beauty and affection. Horace and Alexandra understand Birdie, they have some of the same longings."[13] Hellman, who portrayed the character of Birdie, after her mother, said that she "had meant people to smile at, and to sympathize with, the sad, weak Birdie and certainly I had not meant them to cry."[14]

Horace Giddens, Regina's husband and a member of the fallen aristocracy, represents the people, who allows the Hubbards to take over. Horace works for them and makes money for them and for himself before his illness forces him to soul searching. When once he is brought home from Baltimore, he refuses to participate in what he considers to be the destructive scheme to bring in northern industry and its concomitant evils. Horace predicts that whites and blacks will be turned against each other when the mill is in operation and will take even lower pay. He says: "You can save little money that way, Ben, and make them hate each other just a little more than they do now." (177) Horace opens his eyes in the end and outwits Regina but at the cost of his life. He sincerely tries to save Alexandra from the wicked and 'cunning foxes.'

Addie, who, in a way, speaks for the Negro, is carefully, sparsely, beautifully sketched. Addie is helpless because she is a servant and moreover a black. But still, Addie predicts the decline of the town owing to industrialization and comments on the nefarious means whereby the Hubbards come into wealth and power and indirectly encourages Alexandra to escape from the claws of Hubbards. Hellman makes Addie voice the central theme of the spoilers when she says:

> There are people who eat the earth and eat all the people on it like in the *Bible*, with the locusts. And other people who stand around and watch them eat it. Sometimes I think it ain't right to stand and watch them do it. (188)

The significance of this comment is understood only at the end of the play, when Alexandra repeats it to her mother. The special pleading of Addie's introduction in the play is resolved by Hellman, into a simple, almost casual line of dialogue. When Horace tells her that he is going to leave her something when he dies, Addie answers: "Don't you do that, Mr. Horace. A nigger woman in a white man's will, I'd never get it no how!" (190)

Alexandra, daughter of Regina, is a new woman who resists her mother's ways and walks out on the Hubbards. She is an independent woman who frees herself from the pattern of maternal love and the threat of marriage with Leo. Hellman said that "in Alexandra, she meant to half mock [her] own youthful high-class innocence."[15]

Alexandra is perceived as a commodity for exchange in a business venture of the Hubbards. Just as Oscar bought Birdie, along with Lionnet, the Hubbards think of acquiring Alexandra along with the business. But unlike Birdie, who stays back in her cage, Alexandra escapes the imprisonment of the Hubbards. According to O'Hara, "She is of a new generation with some of the old ways and some of the new ways in her the best of each."[16]

At the beginning of the play, Alexandra is very innocent. She is not aware of the machinations taking place in the household. Bigsby observes that "the only character that stands from the corruption is Regina's daughter, Alexandra.'"[17]

But, gradually, Alexandra turns out to be a clever girl. The conversation between Birdie and Alexandra reveals Alexandra's independent nature. She is a girl of her own will and nobody can make her do anything against her will. She is not timid and weak like Birdie, but is bold and strong. O'Hara thinks: "The thorough bred strain is dominant in Alexandra, but through most of the play, her mother and her uncles confuse docility with weakness, eventually they can no more manage Alexandra than they can change them."[18]

After her father's arrival, Alexandra fusses around him taking good care of his health. In spite of her care and concern, her father dies as a poor victim of her mother's brutality and callousness. When Alexandra sees her father lying dead on the staircase, she asks her mother: "What was papa doing on the staircase?" (203) She is suspicious of her father's death and is determined to find the cause and, in spite of her mother's entreaties, remains firm. Her father's death acts as a catalyst which changes Alexandra from a gay, happy, teenage girl into a shrewd and mature woman.

All of a sudden, Alexandra realizes the horror of her situation and escapes in time. Alexandra is provided with emotional support not only by her father whom she admires, but also by two other women—Birdie, her aunt and Addie, her old black servant. It is Horace's intention that Zan leaves and for that reason, he changes his will so that she will have her own money with which to start a new life, away from the Hubbards. Alexandra tells her mother, Regina:

> Mama, because I want to leave here I've never wanted anything in my life before. Because now I understand what papa was trying to tell me. All in one day: Addie said there were people who ate the earth and other people who stood around and watched them do it. And just now uncle Ben said the same thing. Really, he said the same thing. Well, tell him for me, Mama, I'm not going to stand around and watch you do it. I'll be fighting as hard as he'll be fighting . . . some place else. (206)

Listening to the daughter's challenge, Regina realizes that she has lost her for ever. Although it is by no means 'a call to action' in the manner of Odets's closing speeches, Alexandra's escape from her mother and the reasons she gives for wanting to escape represent the hope for a better world, the hope for the future. In an interview in the *Paris Review*, years later, Lillian Hellman said: "Alexandra was to have become maybe a spinsterish social worker, disappointed another angry young woman."[19] Winfred Dusenbury feels that in creating Alexandra's character, Hellman made "a humanitarian with the tenderness of Birdie and forcefulness of Regina, who arises to sound a new war cry."[20] Small wonder, therefore, if Alexandra is the most admired of all Hellman's characters.

The Little Foxes is an extremely realistic play. As Allen Lewis points out, "Hellman's strength lies in the dramatic power she can extract from the realistic form."[21] The method that Hellman adopts is 'straightforward Realism.' She wants her characters, particularly Hubbards, to be representative of something beyond themselves. We sense that we are seeing the old south as it truly was at the turn of the century. We recognize in the Hubbards the fascists who had begun to devour the earth. We find in the defeated Birdie, decayed European aristocracy, in the dying banker Horace, European capitalism too weak to intervene effectively and in young Alexandra, hope that America would fight.

The Little Foxes offers a highly realistic portrayal of the Hubbards—Ben, Oscar and Regina—who are based on real people. A general quality of Hellman's playwriting is her use of biographical detail. Hellman's mother, Julia Newhouse, is Birdie. Her black nurse, Sophronia, is reflected in her portrait of the black servant, Addie in *The Little Foxes*. With the publication of *Pentimento*, it was revealed that the Hubbards were indeed inspired by Hellman's mother's family who were wealthy Southerners. Making the play Ibsen-like, Hellman worked over a play again and again until the characters were sharp and real.

A close study of the play reveals that the social implications go beyond the story of the Hubbards. For instance, as Richard Watts observes, "Through its thoughtful indignation, *The Little Foxes* becomes a scornful and heartfelt parable of the rise of the industrial South in all its ruthlessness, its savage sense of realism and its fine scorn for the older trappings of Confederate romanticism."[22] The play admirably reflects the devastating effects of those socio-economic changes in both the old families and the wealthy new families.

Ultimately, *The Little Foxes* may be interpreted as a rational assessment of the historical forces it dramatizes. Given its dramatic premises, the play stringently adheres to causality and probability and thus reflects the spirit of objectivity which Emile Zola considered imperative to dramatic realism. The final scene prominently manifests this rational process by offering no facile resolution of the complex moral conflict which structures the play or of the democratic dilemma which that conflict represents. Thus, Hellman's rational process serves to strengthen the validity of play's moral stance. As Eatman observes, "by a synthesis of rational formulation and moral commitment, *The Little Foxes* gains particular authority in casting an image of American destiny—the continuing dialectic of the privileges versus the responsibilities of liberal democracy."[23]

We must remember that *The Little Foxes* was produced at the end of a committed decade in which the writer was pressed to declare his or her allegiance in ideological terms. The play reflects almost all of the anger and frustration of social playwrights of the thirties felt toward the corrupt forces of the power-conscious and exploitative middle class and it does so as an explosive and dynamic work of dramatic art.

Then, as a dramatic expression of Hellman's political views, *The Little Foxes* may be considered as an action on capitalism. Its essential reductivist politics can be described as tenets within the Marxist doctrine—the conflict of base and superstructure, the exposure of social Darwinism, the condemnation of capitalist self interest, the view of an alternative world by some of its characters in rebellion against their harsh surroundings.

To heighten the dramatic effect of the play, Hellman employs not only the realistic and satiric mode of presentation, but also the ironic, a dramatic device, that calls for an objective and amused detachment. Through the dramatic device of irony, Hellman raises the level of impersonation in the play by giving us characters—Ben and Regina—who assume roles when dealing with other people. They playact above the level of simple impersonation of the character by an actor and we have the character assuming a hypocritical role. The character of Ben is ironic whose ruthless exercise of power is frequently funny as it catches the irony that in this society undisguised malevolence can be more effective than guilt—weakened underhandedness.

We have another kind of irony in characters who have knowledge other characters lack and who consequently speak ironically. Regina explains Ben to Oscar. Ben explains Regina. They talk for his benefit. There are situations where one or more characters are conscious of the ironies produced by ironic words and visible means a sense of cross-purposes.

Enclosing these ironies is dramatic irony. The audience

knows more than the characters. In *The Little Foxes*, we know before Ben and Oscar that Regina knows about the bonds. We know before Regina that Ben and Oscar don't need Horace's money and we realize that Horace is charting his own doom when he repeatedly says that Regina will not have her way as long as he is alive.

Hellman also employs what is known as boomerang irony to achieve the satiric effect. The stolen bonds which temporarily free Ben and Oscar from Regina put them in her control when Horace dies. And Regina, apparently freeing herself completely by allowing Horace to die, is left at the end with the threat of disclosure when Alexandra questions the death place of her father. This question arouses Ben's suspicion. Even Horace's effort to outwit Regina boomerangs. His threat to make a new will leaving only the bonds to Regina causes his death.

Like any great dramatic artist, Hellman makes use of imagery in her attempt to achieve artistic excellence. She employs a strong 'Darwinian imagery' of the jungle, to express the concern of the Hubbards for the mad pursuits of money and success. Hellman actually makes no direct reference to Nature or Garden of Eden except in the implied meaning in her title—*The Little Foxes*. By doing so, she gives to her view of life a pattern and a design which is related, in a way to the original myth of Eden. Each member of the Hubbard family is an animal in a lawless jungle where he is expected to look out for himself. Oscar advises his son Leo: "It's everyman's duty to think of himself." (164)

The Hubbards in their avarice and rapacity are like 'the little foxes that spoil our Vines: for our Vines have tender grapes'—an image that was evoked by a description in the *Bible* (Song of Solomon II, 15). Like the Snopses of Faulkner and Babbitt of Sinclair Lewis, the Hubbards are the new generation of animalistic Adams who are ruthlessly exploiting and destroying the innocence and weakness of the lesser animals of the jungle. The situation is slightly redeemed by people like Alexandra who declares at the end that she will fight those who eat up the earth and its people like the locusts.

Hellman adds another jungle image to the play in her description of the Hubbard family as 'a nest of particularly vicious diamond-back rattle-snakes.' In this kind of vicious set-up, the loss of an original arcadia is symbolized by the cotton estate, Lionnet, that was once owned by Birdie's family. As Birdie described it: "The lawn was so smooth all the way down to the river, with the trims of zinnias and red-feather plush. And the figs and blue little plums and the scuppernongs." (150) Symbolically, the 'little foxes' have plundered this fruitful garden and destroyed its 'tender vines.'

The Little Foxes is laudable for its stage-worthiness. The play conforms so perfectly to the nature of theatre. Although one may never have seen the play performed, one knows how it will look and sound on stage. Hellman has an instinctive sense of rhythm, knowing when to accelerate the action and when to let it subside. She excels at group scenes which intimidate most playwrights because they find it difficult to achieve the multiple rhythms that such scenes require.

The first act of *The Little Foxes* begins with an exchange between two domestics—then the rhythm accelerates as Birdie enters, babbling excitedly. When her husband, Oscar, checks her effusions, the pace slackens. As Regina enters with her brothers and their guest, Mr. Marshall, the conversation proceeds evenly for the purpose of exposition. Gradually the pace quickens as Ben describes the rise of the Hubbards in the rhetoric of conquest, boasting that his family wrested Lionnet, the plantation, from their owners. To divert sympathy to Birdie, who has just been described as chattel, Hellman balances Ben's swinish oratory with a gesture of courtesy from Marshall: "May I bring you a glass of port, Mrs. Hubbard?" (145)

No scene in *The Little Foxes* is gratuitous. Leo's theft of the bonds comes as no surprise because Regina had alluded earlier to his petty thievery. When Oscar slaps Birdie, it is not merely to stun the audience. A man who wantonly kills animals could easily mistreat his wife, especially when there are no witnesses. When Alexandra remarks that her father's medicine bottle must not break, the question in the audience's mind is not 'will it break?' but 'how will it break?' What seems to be chance events must be motivated dramatically so that the accidental becomes an extension of character. Crucial to the plot are the bonds Leo steals from Horace's safe-deposit box. Horace must learn of the theft, as he does, in a perfectly natural way. He sends for the box because he wishes to draw up a new will. The medicine bottle must break and Regina must make no effort to replace it. Horace drops it immediately after Regina tells him that she despises him. Thus, every scene comes naturally to conform the play to the stage enactability.

Though a brilliant, sardonic comedy like Ben Jonson's *Volpone*, *The Little Foxes* has more often than not been mistaken for a melodrama by some critics. For instance, J.W. Krutch feels that "in view of the violence of the actions, *The Little Foxes* be called a melodrama, which ends with the triumph of villiany."[24] William T. Going in his "Essays on Alabama Literature" comments that "Hellman, by avoiding 'happy ending' may save her plays from an indiscriminate labelling of melodrama, but despite the concern of her main characters with basic moral issues, the outcome is not quite the tragedy that offers resolution to emotional tension, nor is the ending inevitable in a Sophoclean sense."[25] Even the most notable critic of Hellman, C.W.E. Bigsby, in his compact study of American drama, noted that "*The Little Foxes* is a melodrama."[26]

But a close reading of the play reveals that *The Little Foxes* is not a melodrama. It is true that it has a certain melodramatic quality. Any intensely exciting stage action developed primarily for the sake of a thrill and strong emotional impact through terror, shock, fear, or suspense is melodramatic. As Lederer observes: "when one thinks of melodrama, one thinks of a play with artificially heightened emotion . . . and improbable turn of plot, leading to a conventionally happy ending with vice punished and virtue rewarded."[27]

But *The Little Foxes* does not fit the definition. No doubt, *The Little Foxes* makes successful use of scenes of melodrama that are natural, acceptable parts of drama itself. They arise from established character and situation and further the movement of the play without distraction. Two important scenes are vividly melodramatic. The first begins in Act II with the tense exchange between Regina and Horace and ends in the violent upstairs argument while the other jungle beasts plan to divide the spoils. The second is, of course, the heart attack, a harrowing event of pure melodrama from the start of the argument through the broken bottle and the collapse on the stairs.

But these scenes of melodrama are skilfully used so as to further the effect of a realistic style. So, the use of melodramatic scenes need not necessarily make *The Little Foxes* a melodrama. This is made clear to us by Hellman herself when she says:

> I almost meant *The Little Foxes* to be a kind of dramatic comedy. . . . I think most villains are funny. . . . I was amazed to find much about *The Little Foxes* that I hadn't intended—aristocracy against the middle class and so on. I had meant the audience to recognize some part of themselves in the money dominated Hubbards: I had not meant people to think of them as villains, to whom they had no connection. I began to think that greed and the cheating that is its usual companion were, comic as well as evil.[28]

It is at once interesting and profitable to draw a parallel between *The Little Foxes* and other plays of the contemporary playwrights—Chekhov, Strindberg, Arthur Miller, Tennessee Williams, Clifford Odets and Kafka. *The Little Foxes* is, in many senses, close to Chekhov's *The Cherry Orchard.* Both plays are concerned with dispossession, with the collapse of old myths and the denial of supposed verities. Just as Lophakin in *The Cherry Orchard*, Ben in *The Little Foxes* announces that he had bought the family plantation Lionnet along with their daughter Birdie. The only difference is Lophakin is an ambiguous figure, willing to destroy the old cherry orchard in order to build villas for the rising bourgeoisie, but showing respect and compassion for those he is displacing whereas the Hubbards are single-mindedly cruel.

The similarity between the Hubbards of Bowden and Vaidens of Florence in Strindberg's *The Store* is striking. Both families's store is the key to their acquisition of decaying plantations of the aristocracy, both families's fortune is founded on theft and profiteering, both families seek through marriage social respectability and acceptance. Just as Miltiades Vaiden marries Synda to acquire the appurtenances of aristocracy, so does Oscar Hubbard marry Birdie to possess their land.

Hellman's *The Little Foxes* is also reminiscent of Arthur Miller's *All My Sons* as a social drama. Both plays dramatize the sinful acts of parents and the coming of age of idealistic offspring who ultimately feel they must separate themselves from the tarnished world of their elders. The protagonist of Hellman's *The Little Foxes*, Regina Giddens, and the protagonist of Miller's *All My Sons*, Joe Keller, are both preoccupied with money. In their efforts to acquire it, however, both commit misdeeds that their children cannot forgive—Regina sins against society as well as the family; Miller's Joe Keller also sins both against society and the institution of the family. Not only are Regina and Joe parallel figures, but so are Alexandra and Joe's son Chris. Both plays conclude with a dramatic confrontation between the parent and the child.

More obvious than the similarities between *The Little Foxes* and *All My Sons* are the parallels between *The Little Foxes* and the two plays of Tennessee Williams's *The Glass Menagerie* and *A Streetcar Named Desire*. As William Wright has implied, "Williams, like Hellman a Southern Writer, might well have based two of his most memorable Southern female characters, Amanda Wingfield and Blanche Dubois, on Hellman's fragile, alcoholic Birdie."[29] It is precisely the combination of silliness and pathos that one finds in Hellman's Birdie which is also seen in Williams's Amanda and Blanche. Also reminiscent of *The Little Foxes* is Amanda's warning to Laura that unless she makes an effort to control her life, she will end up helpless and dependent, just as Birdie's warning to Alexandra. In Williams's *Streetcar Named Desire*, Blanche recollects the loss of family plantation, as Hellman's Birdie does in *The Little Foxes*. Hellman's use of South as setting, the character types she introduces, her creation of various speech patterns to differentiate her characters, and her pungent blend of humour, pathos and irony are also found in Williams's plays.

Hellman's *The Little Foxes* can also be compared to and contrasted with Odets's *Awake and Sing*. Hellman's realism in *The Little Foxes* has an historical setting in the rural South while Odets's is contemporary, urban and Jewish. Hellman deals with the agents of social injustice as well as their victims, while Odets is concerned only with the latter. In spite of the difference between the dramatic worlds, these two plays share a dramatic pattern by which each puts family struggles at the service of an indictment of social and political conditions. In both plays, the destructive family is dominated by strong mother, who is in some sense villainous and against whom the father is ineffective. Again, in both the plays, the death of a father figure, who knows truer values but cannot act, educates and liberates the young person. Both plays have a triumphant resolution in which the young person declares opposition to the family's values.

Yet another play that stands comparison with Hellman's *The Little Foxes* is Kafka's *Metamorphosis*. In *Metamorphosis*, the story of a man's change into an insect, Kafka interprets human psychology in terms of animal symbols. Kafka's pathos is the pathos of loneliness and exclusion from the family and, beyond that, the estrangement of man from his human environment. Although Regina has not the self-recognition of herself that the hero of *Metamorphosis* has, and so does not appear to herself as a despicable insect, it can be questioned whether in a sequel to *The Little Foxes*, she might not have some self-revulsion, for there is a challenge in her young daughter's last words. Certainly by this time, Regina is suffering from a feeling of estrangement from everyone from whom she normally might expect affection.

Thus, *The Little Foxes* is a powerful and fascinating play and a highly charged theatrical experience. Better crafted than Hellman's other works, it is varied in characterization and language. The play is effective because of the humanity of its inhuman characters. It successfully combines Hellman's powers of dramatic entertainment and social concern into a play which so completely captivates its audience and so decisively makes its point.

NOTES

1. Lillian Hellman, *The Little Foxes* in *The Collected Plays* (Boston-Toronto: Little, Brown, 1971), p. 152.
2. D. Virginia Falk, *Lillian Hellman* (New York: Alfred & Knopf, 1978), p. 54.
3. Richard Lockridge, *Sunday*, February 16, 1939, cited in Katherine Lederer, *Lillian Hellman* (Boston: Twayne, 1979), p. 43.
4. Sam Smiley, "The Drama of Attack," *Didactic Plays of the American Depression* (Columbia: University of Missouri Press, 1972), p. 59.
5. Katherine Lederer (Boston: Twayne, 1979), p. 48.
6. Allen Lewis, *American Plays and Playwrights of the Contemporary Theatre* (New York: Crown, 1970), p. 106.
7. Lillian Hellman, Richard G. Stern, "An Interview with Lillian Hellman," 1958, *Conversations with Lillian Hellman*, ed. Jackson R. Bryer (University Press of Mississippi, 1986), p. 35.
8. Lillian Hellman, Fred Gardner, "An Interview with Lillian Hellman," 1968, *Conservations with Lillian Hellman*, p. 116.
9. Malcom Goldstein, *The Political Stage: American Drama and Theatre in the Great Depression* (New York: Oxford University Press, 1974), p. 36.
10. Lillian Hellman, *Herald Tribune*, September 24, 1939, cited in Katherine Lederer, p. 42.
11. C.W.E. Bigsby, "Lillian Hellman," *A Critical Introduction to Twentieth Century American Drama* (Cambridge University Press, 1982), p. 280.
12. O'Hara, *Today in American Drama* (New York: Greenwood Press, 1969), p. 84.
13. Falk, *Lillian Hellman*, p. 54.
14. Lillian Hellman, *Pentimento*, p. 180, cited in Katherine Lederer, p. 39.
15. Lillian Hellman, *Pentimento*, p. 182, cited in Katherine Lederer, p. 45.
16. O'Hara, p. 85.
17. C.W.E. Bigsby, p. 281.
18. O'Hara, p. 85.
19. Lillian Hellman, "Interview with Lillian Hellman: The Art of the Theatre I," *Paris Review*, Vol. 33, Issue No. 37, Winter,

1965, pp. 64-65.

20. Winfred L. Dusenbury "Socioeconomic Forces," *The Theme of Loneliness in Modern American Drama* (University of Florida Press, 1960), pp. 113-54.
21. Allen Lewis, *American Plays and Playwrights of the Contemporary Theatre* (New York: Crown, 1970), p. 107.
22. Richard Watts, Junior, *The Best Plays of 1938-1939*, cited in Winfred L. Dusenbury, pp. 113-54.
23. James Eastman, *Players*, December 1972-January 1973, p. 73.
24. Joseph Wood Krutch, *Nation*, December 26, 1936, pp. 769-70.
25. William. T. Going, "Essays on Alabama Literature," *Prestons and Hubbards* (New York: Crown, 1970), p. 152.
26. C.W.E. Bigsby, p. 280.
27. Lederer Katherine, p. 41.
28. Lillian Hellman, *Pentimento*, pp. 180-82. Cited in Katherine Lederer, *Lillian Hellman* (Boston: Twayne, 1979), p. 39.
29. William Wright, *Lillian Hellman: The Image—The Woman* (New York: Simon and Schuster, 1986), p. 301.

The Malignancy of Nazism: *Watch on the Rhine*

Widely hailed as the best of the anti-Nazi dramas, *Watch on the Rhine* (1940) is the most human, the warmest, and, in some ways, the most understanding of all Hellman's plays. It is an American political drama, arguing against American isolationism during World War II. It is a vital, eloquent and compassionate play about an American family suddenly awakened to the danger threatening their liberty. It is a moving story about the betrayal of a resistance worker by a cynical German exile. The play asserts the necessity of struggle against both evil and the passivity of bystanders.

Watch on the Rhine concerns itself with the theme of ethical responsibility, a theme also touched upon in *The Searching Wind*. Here, Hellman turns to the current political situation in order to awaken the Americans to the growing menace of fascism. The title of the play, taken from a German marching song, suggests that Nazism must be watched and fought not only in Europe but in the U.S. Accordingly, Hellman brings the anti-fascist struggle into an upper-class American home.

Hellman's prescient dramatization of the slow-awakening of an American family to the realities of Nazism is depicted powerfully. The enemy is not capitalism, or the privileged members of society, but fascism at its melodramatic worst. Hellman chooses *Watch on the Rhine* as the framework for the expression of the European tragedy and of the hidden sense of guilt which those who were too much outside it will never lose. The malignancy of Nazism played out by a group of German refugees and Nazis in the United States and a non-Jewish German anti-Nazi activist who leaves the safety of the U.S. to return to Germany to resume clandestine anti-Nazi work is depicted with skill in

Watch on the Rhine.

Watch on the Rhine is set in a spacious home, twenty miles from Washington D.C., where dowager Fanny Farrelly lives with her bachelor son, David Farrelly. It is an average American middle-class family. The first act opens with one group of characters—a black Butler Joseph, French house-keeper Anise, wealthy dowager Fanny Farrelly and her son David who are anxiously awaiting the arrival of Sara, the daughter of Fanny, her husband Kurt Muller and their children. The gravity of their anxiety is revealed in the conversation between Anise and Fanny:

Anise: (Looking at the watch) It's now twenty seven minutes before nine. It will be impossible to continue telling you the time every three minutes from now until Miss Sara arrives. I think you are having a nervous breakdown. Compose yourself.

Fanny: It's been twenty years. Any mother would be nervous. If your daughter were coming home and you had not seen her and a husband and grand children.[1]

Fanny Farrelly is the widow of a liberal judge and diplomat to whose memory she constantly refers and whose portrait hangs on the living room wall throughout the play. Fanny has been an arbitrary dictator over her son, David, and she would have been one over her daughter, Sara, if Sara had not declared her independence twenty years ago by marrying a German, Kurt Muller.

Sara arrives with her anti-fascist husband, Kurt Muller, who fought in Spain as well as in Germany, and also with their children Joshuwa, Bodo and Babette. Kurt's family arrives hungry and ill-clothed at the Farrelly mansion. Kurt carries the marks of torture by fascists—scars and broken hands. Kurt tells Fanny that he was 'an anti-fascist, and that does not pay well.' Although Fanny and David cannot understand the fanatic political consecration of Kurt which has caused much physical suffering and hardship to himself and his family, they greet him warmly and attempt to make him and his family feel at home. Kurt explains to Fanny how he became an anti-fascist:

> On that day I saw twenty seven men murdered in a Nazi street-fight. I say, I cannot just stand by now and watch. My time has come to move. (Looks down, smiles). I say with Luther 'Here I stand. I can do nothing else. God help me. Amen.' (233)

Kurt has managed to bring his wife and children to visit her mother and brother. But, he himself is on a mission—he is carrying $23,000 in cash, collected from 'the pennies of the poor who do not like fascism.' He will soon have to leave his family in Washington and take the money back to Europe where it is needed to free other anti-Nazi prisoners.

Staying with the Farrellys when the Mullers arrive are a different group and breed of Europeans—Romanian Count Teck de-Brancovis and his wife Marthe. Teck is a Nazi sympathizer and a gambler—a professional Romanian aristocrat. Marthe has lived in Europe most of her life and dislikes Nazis. The couple is visiting Fanny because Marthe's mother and she were friends. Even while Teck stays at Farrelly's house as guest, at the time of Sara's and Kurt's arrival, he becomes inquisitive about Kurt and wants to know more about him. The marriage of Teck and Marthe has disintegrated. They are in debt and are living on credit. What little money they have is lost in Teck's gambling with his Nazi friends at the German Embassy in Washington. Marthe falls in love with David Farrelly, Fanny's thirty-nine-year-old son. She tries to find a way of leaving her husband.

The conflict, however, is provided by Teck. A weak character and a failure in his own career, he is jealous of Kurt Muller and also sees in him a chance to make a small fortune. Kurt knows Teck's identity and his past, and Teck is suspicious of Kurt. Teck's curiosity becomes more evident towards the end of the first act. When Teck has picked up the brief case of Kurt and is trying the lock, Marthe questions him:

Teck: Wondering why the luggage is unlocked, and a shabby briefcase is so carefully locked.

Marthe: You're curious about Herr Muller.

Teck: Yes. And I do not know why? Something far away. . . . I am curious about a daughter of the Farrellys who marries a German who has bullet scars on his face and broken bones in his hands. (235-36)

At the end of the first act, Marthe warns Teck against harming Kurt. She tells him she will leave him if he makes trouble. The Count discovers the money which Kurt is carrying and figures out Kurt's identity. He pilfers Kurt's luggage for evidence which he takes to the German Embassy and as a result several of Kurt's companions are arrested in Europe. When the news breaks that three prominent anti-fascists have been caught, imprisoned and tortured by. the Nazis, Teck discovers that they are close friends of Kurt and that he is a missing fourth on the Nazis list. Teck tries to blackmail him by threatening to reveal his identity to the Germans:

Teck: (turns, crosses up to get newspaper from the Secretary) It is in the afternoon paper, Herr Muller . . . the Zurich papers today reprinted a despatch from the Berliner Tageblatt—on the capture of Colonel Max Freidank. Freidank is said to be the Chief of the Anti-Nazi underground movement.

Sara: (Crying it out) Max—

Kurt: Be, still, Sara.

Teck: They told me of it at the Embassy last night. They also told me that with him they had taken a man who called himself Ebber and a man who called himself Triste. They could not find a man called Gotter. I shall be a lonely man without Marthe. I am also very poor one. I should like to have ten thousand dollars before I go. (254-55)

At the end of the second act, Teck asks Marthe to leave with him. But she refuses, saying:

> You won't believe it, because you can't believe anything that hasn't got tricks to it, but David hasn't much to do with this. I told you I would leave some day, and I remember where I said it and why I said it. (252)

Soon Kurt finds himself at the complete mercy of Teck. Kurt tells Fanny and David that Teck has discovered the $23,000 he is carrying gathered from the poor anti-Nazis. When Fanny asks whether it is not careless of him to leave twenty three thousand dollars going around to be seen, Kurt answers:

> No, it was not careless of me. It is in a locked briefcase. I have thus carried money for many years. There seemed no safer place than Sara's home. It was careless of you to have in your house a man who opens baggage and blackmails. (257)

Here Hellman's parable is clear. The confrontation between pro and anti-Nazis literally enters an American parlour as the refugees force their hosts to take sides.

David and Fanny take the first step towards joining Kurt's side when they offer to pay Teck themselves. But, they still don't understand the actual situation completely. David tells Kurt that he will be safe and asks him whether his passport is all right. When Kurt says that it is not quite so, Fanny asks why it is not so. Kurt says:

> Because people like me are not given visas with such ease. And I was in a hurry to bring my wife and my children to safety. Madam, Fanny, you must come to understand it is no longer the world you once knew. (258)

Still failing to understand, David tells Kurt: "It doesn't matter. You're political refugee. We don't . . . turn back people like you." (258) Sara says "you don't understand David," (258) and explains that Kurt has to go back to Germany.

In Act III, Teck reads from a German embassy list of wanted men a description of Kurt's underground activities. When Fanny says she is sickened by Teck, Kurt makes a key speech:

> Fanny and David are Americans and they do not understand our world—as yet. (Turns to David and Fanny) All Fascists

> are not of one mind. There are those who give the orders, those who carry out the orders, those who watch the orders being carried out. Then there are those who are half in, half hoping to come in. (265)

When Fanny and David leave the room to get the money, Teck says:

> The New World has left the room. We are Europeans, born to trouble and understanding it. . . . They are young. The world has gone well for most of them. For us—we are, like peasants watching the big forest. Work, trouble, ruin—But no need to call curses at the forest. There it is, it will be again, always—for us. (268)

Kurt at first promises to comply, but he knows that cooperation with the unprincipled Teck is useless. Only violence can resolve the situation. When Fanny leaves the room to get the money, Kurt attacks Teck and knocks him unconscious. With gun in hand, Kurt carries Teck out to the garden, where he shoots him. After Kurt kills Teck, he says: "I have a great hate for the violent: They are sick of the world. Maybe I am sick now, too." (272)

Sara knows what is happening and knows that it is inevitable. She calls the airline and reserves a seat for Kurt under another name on the next plane to Texas where he will cross over to Mexico and then to Europe. When Kurt returns from the garden, they explain to Fanny and David, who come to understand that Kurt has done what he had to do. The killing of Teck was an act of war, except that "when you kill in a war, it is not so lonely." (272) Indignant at Teck's perfidy, Farrellys are nevertheless shocked at first by his act but finally realize that evil based on violence, that is, Nazism, can be fought only on its own terms.

A man of peace driven to murder to protect the cause he is fighting for, Kurt says to his children as he prepares to leave them, in a touching farewell scene:

> The world is out of shape, we said, when there are hungry men. And until it gets in shape, men will always steal and lie and (a little more slowly) kill. But for whatever reason it is done, and whoever does it—you understand me—it is all bad. I want you to remember that whoever does it, it is bad. (275)

Fanny and David make their decision when Kurt tells them that they can either phone the police or wait for two days to give him a headstart, making themselves, in effect, accessories to murder. Fanny and David give Kurt their support. The children and Sara will stay with them there with little hope that Kurt will ever return. Kurt leaves and Sara goes upstairs to comfort the children. At the end of the play, Fanny tells David: "We are shaken out of the magnolias, eh?" (276) David asks her if she understands that they are going to be in for trouble. Fanny replies in a line reminiscent of *The Little Foxes*, but spoken to a much different purpose: "I understand it very well, we will manage. I am not put together with flour paste. And neither are you—I am happy to learn." (276)

Hellman says in *Penimento* that this is her purpose to write *Watch on the Rhine*: "to write a play about nice, liberal Americans whose lives would be shaken up by Europeans, by a world the new Fascists had won because the old values had long been dead."[2]

Watch on the Rhine offers a fine contrast between two ways of living—American and European. While cloaking in nobility of spirit, the European and American sensibilities are strongly contrasted to make a cogent point about the difficulty of living in compromise. Kurt Muller and his three children represent the European maturity and experience in the midst of Nazi evil. As against these, the American Fanny Farrelly and her son, David, live in a strange insularity. The Farrellys not only do not understand, but also, don't care that the world is up in flames. In their nineteenth century attitudes, life still consists of breakfast on the terrace and love intrigues in high society. Moreover, they do not understand Muller's poverty. One of the Muller boys has sensed this: "Grandma has not seen much of the world." (241) Referring to the American ignorance of the Nazi evil, Kurt remarks: "Fanny and David are Americans and they do not understand our world—as yet." (265)

The life that the Farrellys lead is easy and luxurious, secure and comfortable in the American style. They know the world in a way, the American way, though they are by no means prepared for what comes to them from Europe, which amounts to saying they know the world very little. For all their contacts with the world, abroad and with Washington, the capital of the U.S., and for all the number of words they must have heard and read on international subjects, they still have the American innocence of what Europe is like, of what European living is and of what Europeans are. This American family now must pass through the classic pattern of American involvement with European fascism, first failure to recognise its existence, second failure to see it as a personal threat and third appeasement.

Then, we can also see a sharp contrast between two sets of European and American marriages. Hellman does create in Mullers something like a successful family whose bonds are not merely those of flesh and blood but of an implicit, never-spoken of and perpetual act of faith. The second set of marriage of Teck and Marthe disintegrates. Marthe married Teck at seventeen to fulfil her mother's fantasies. Now only Teck's threats hold this marriage together. Marthe falls in love with David Farrelly, who has previously flirted with her, but after the realization of European honour, accepts her sincerely.

The plot of *Watch on the Rhine* is not so tightly constructed as those of Hellman's previous plays—*The Children's Hour* and *The Little Foxes*. The dragged first-half consists of over-emotional padding, but most critics describe it as 'pleasantly discursive' or 'spontaneous' and 'witty.'

The first act is a cliche and shows the wit and broad humour of the characterization and actions. One group of characters are anxiously awaiting the arrival of another group of characters. In expressing anticipation and anxiety, they provide the audience with details about the new arrivals. When the guests arrive, we have a fine family 'recognition scene' of the good people, full of happy surprises and further information. This is followed by an ominous scene of suspected recognition between two old enemies. The act concludes with evil just about to get the upper hand over good, before the intermission in which the audience can relish its suspense. This mechanical structure continues in the subsequent act, through a series of confrontations, crises and resolutions between various characters ending in a climactic confrontation and catastrophic denouement but on a lofty note.

Some critics feel that *Watch on the Rhine* is somewhat faulty in structure. For instance, Rosamind Gilder remarks: "Hellman's exposition is slow in *Watch on the Rhine* and her sub-plot is cumbersome. She does not come to grips with her subject till well on in the second act and she permits herself a number of lapses from the probable."[3] However, the same critic feels that "yet with these faults the play, in its authentic passages, has so successfully translated into dramatic terms a fundamental human ideal that its shortcomings are forgotten."[4] Brooks Atkinson is of the view that "the narrative of *Watch on the Rhine* drifts into generalities before the main action is well started." But again he praises the play as a whole saying that "commenting the plot is only carping at technicalities, and it does not destroy a general impression that *Watch on the Rhine* is the finest thing she has written."[5] With all its shortcomings, we may concur with Basil Wright when he says: "Apart from a slightly machine-made opening to the first act, the author manipulates her plot and characters with an assurance, an economy and a sense of human values to which only an exceptionally talented cast could do justice."[6]

The 'exceptionally talented cast' in *Watch on the Rhine* reveals Hellman's remarkable gift for characterization. The various characters in the play are observed with a keen eye to the exact kind of detail that will convince us of their actual existence and difference in their relationships and mutual reactions to each other. The characters are also well-drawn out of affection for people of integrity. The writing is enormously skilful, humorous, witty and also forthright when the time comes for plain speaking.

In fact, the whole action of *Watch on the Rhine* stems from the characters themselves and their relations to the world around them. They take on a life of their own and at times their speeches seem to come only through the author's fingertips. This shows how the characters are alive and integrated in the author's mind. Hellman draws a vivid contrast between the simple goodwill of a normal American family—Fanny Farrelly and David Farrelly—and the dark callousness of Europeans—Kurt Muller and Sara and their three children, and also the evil Teck de-Brancovis and his wife Marthe—who have grown accustomed to intrigue and desperation.

Kurt Muller, the protagonist of the play, is modelled on Julia, a childhood friend of Hellman.[7] He is about forty-three, a good looking former engineer, who, having left Germany in 1933, has become an outstanding fighter against Nazism in Germany and against the insidious spread of fascism throughout the world. Julia, the model for the character of Kurt Muller, herself, was a saintly woman who shared her wealth with the poor and lost a leg and finally her life in the fight against fascism. Just like her, Kurt's hands are also broken, his face is scarred when he and his family enter Fanny Farrelly's house.

Hellman makes Kurt Muller a radical and an anti-fascist for the justice of his cause. Her task is to make the American opponent of World War I and a German national and a likely Communist, and create a hero with whom American audiences can identify. To do this, she invests him with typical American heroic virtues. To begin with, Kurt is a man of action, not talk. Because opportunities to demonstrate anti-Fascist heroism in an upper-class living room are necessarily limited, Hellman assigns the task of explaining Kurt's attitudes to others. When we want to know what Kurt's beliefs are, we need only listen to his children:

Bodo: Did Mama write that Papa was a great hero? He was brave, he was calm, he was expert, he was resourceful, he was—

Kurt: (laughs) My unprejudiced biographer. (227)

Bodo: He likes to know how each thing of everything is put together. And he is so fond of being clean. (234)

In the character of Kurt, Hellman draws a rounded and appealing being, a man at once heroic and human, brave and fearful. Kurt is by nature thoughtful, peace-loving, gentle and compassionate. He hates violence. His mind is repelled by brutality. His nerves cry out against pain. That is why, the character of Kurt, the resistance fighter, has received utmost attention by critics. For instance, Katherine Lederer says that Kurt is the lone protagonist "not only because Hellman wrote the role with passion and admiration but because he acts with decision and courage and is Hellman's most eloquent spokesman for human rights and liberty."[8] Rosamind Gilder says how Kurt becomes the prototype of all those who, like Hamlet, revolt against the cursed spite that calls upon them to set right by violence a world gone out of joint.[9] Barret H. Clark succinctly sums up Kurt's character when he says: "Kurt, the little German who gives up his work, his wife, children and is ready to give up his life in order to crush what threatens all we believe in, could scarcely have been anything but sympathetic."[10]

If Kurt is an anti-fascist, Teck is a Nazi sympathizer and a gambler.[11] He is a somewhat mysterious and penniless Romanian Count. He is presented as an effete German aristocrat and is offered as representative of those who had seen Hitler's rise as offering an opportunity for their own aggrandizement. He is a world-adventurer, not the direct Nazi, but the assiduous jackal, the Nazi type without the Nazi faith.

Teck is obviously presented as the antithesis to Kurt. He is a Dracula challenging Kurt's Parsifal, acknowledging no commitment beyond himself. Both Teck and Kurt make judgements about National Socialism. Whereas Kurt correctly evaluates its evil and enlists in the fight against it, Teck under-estimates Nazi strength. Kurt rightly interprets him:

> [Some Fascists] come late; some because they did not jump in time, some because they were stupid, some because they were shocked at the crudity of the German evil, and preferred their own evil and some because they were fastidious men. For those last, we may well some day have pity. They

are lost men, their spoils are small, their day is past. (265)

But Teck is clever, patient and ruthless. He wants only to be on the winning side. And he will not play his hand recklessly. In spite of his cleverness and schemy nature, Teck gets killed by Kurt Muller. Teck is no more than a pitiful little rat, himself a victim.

But Hellman wastes no hatred upon him. She even goes out of her way to make Teck understandable and she likewise endows him with some remnants of human decency. Teck is not quite an active evil figure. His corruption grows directly out of the passivity and cowardice of his half-commitment to fascist activities. Teck exploits others only to gain acceptance by the Nazis. In the words of Barret H. Clark, "Hellman has learned that to symbolize a situation it is not necessary to assume the manner or dramatize the gestures of contempt. The fact speaks for itself when the fact is wholly and understandingly embodied in speech and action."[12]

Thus, the two European men, Kurt and Teck, are contrasted. Kurt Muller is a full-length hero, a man who works for others. He is articulate in a wholly winning manner and he goes out of his way to stress his unimportance. Whereas Teck de-Brancovis is a villain, the Romanian aristocrat blackmails his hosts into buying him off when he discovers Kurt's identity. Teck is no lay figure; he does not even represent fascism. In this way, the two European men differ completely in their mentality.

Like Kurt and Teck, Sara Muller and Marthe de-Brancovis are sharply contrasted with each other. Although both of them are American-born ladies, they are married to Europeans—Kurt Muller and Teck de-Brancovis respectively. If one is anti-Nazi, the other is Nazi sympathizer. Sara shows immense courage in sending her husband back to Germany to fight for his cause. She is rather proud of his activities. Whereas Sara is proud of her husband, Marthe, who knows her husband's evil nature, develops a kind of hatred towards him.

Fanny Farrelly and her son David make interesting characters. Fanny is the widow of Joshuva Farrelly and she keeps her husband's portrait in the drawing room of her house. As her husband is a liberal judge, Fanny measures everything with his judgement. She bosses over her son David. As bossy as she is, Fanny's wit gives her charm. Part of her function in life is to find out the local gossip and improve on it—'wit it up' and the rest is to keep her family in order according to her own upper-class lights. Though a strong woman, given to raising her voice when she does not get her way, she is generous, loving and liberal. David Farrelly never asserts himself but allows his mother to attempt to make him into his father's image. Hellman makes these two characters develop gradually and become aware of the necessity to take active part in fascist movement. Both Fanny and David assist Kurt whole-heartedly, although they realize that the eventual revelation of the murder will cause trouble for them.

Thus, the characters in *Watch on the Rhine* really carry us along with the play, however much or little the anti-Nazi connotations may stick in our minds. To Hellman's restraint and precise ability at characterization, she adds for the first time in warm emotional feeling within the family which makes *Watch on the Rhine* one of the finest plays to come out of the war years. With the characters portrayed with dignity and taste, the play will always be deeply touching.

Watch on the Rhine is important not only for its memorable characters but also for its intense realism and contemporary relevance. Written in 1940, and produced eight months before Pearl Harbor, the play is understandably more patriotic than eloquent. The rise of Hitler and sadism of the Nazi regime, the brutality of Fascism which Hellman has witnessed in Spain, seemed to her a manifestation on a monstrous scale of the same evil in human nature that motivated the Hubbards. She felt on her return that the people in the United States were but dimly aware of the danger of Nazism to the entire world. She summed up her attitude in a few sentences in *Pentimento*:

> I am a writer, I am also a Jew. I want to be quite sure that I can continue to be a writer, and that if I want to say that

> greed is bad or persecution is worse, I can do so without being branded by the malice of the people making a living by that malice.[13]

And so, she started writing the play, *Watch on the Rhine*.

Watch on the Rhine opened in 1941 when the whole world was being forced to support liberal ideas actively or default into the dynamic religions of Nazism and other forms of fascism. The play brings the subject home fiercely to those Americans who imagined materialism a possibility. Perhaps, the play is offered as an anxious debate about the utility of art at the moments of social crisis. Hence Hellman has one of her characters insist that there is "Too much talk. By this time all of us know where we are and what we have to do. It is an indulgence to sit in a room and discuss your beliefs as if they were the afternoon's golf-game." (240)

Although many critics feel that *Watch on the Rhine* is Hellman's best play, Hellman in her discussions of her work, usually dismissed it as the best anti-Nazi play of the war years. *Watch on the Rhine* has a topical relevance. Brooks Atkinson makes this clearer when he says: "Since Miss Hellman has communicated her thoughts dramatically in terms of articulate human beings, *Watch on the Rhine* ought to be full of meaning a quarter of a century from now when people are beginning to wonder what life was like in America when the Nazi evil began to creep across the sea."[14] Thus, *Watch on the Rhine* has a strong contemporary appeal by virtue of its successful reconstruction of the anti-fascist atmosphere.

In spite of its realistic flavour and authenticity, *Watch on the Rhine* has more often than not been taken for an old-fashioned melodrama by some critics because of the pervasive cruelty and violence in the play. For example, Brendan Gill, reviving the 1980 production of *Watch on the Rhine*, says: "Miss Hellman has always been a champion of the well-made play and it's true that one detects in the net plotting of *Watch on the Rhine*, a taint of melodrama that grows less and less tolerable with age."[15] Leonard Ungar feels: "of all Hellman's plays, *Watch on the*

Rhine comes closest being melodrama of the monochromatic school where the villain is unspeakably black and the hero angelically white."[16]

But a clear understanding of the play reveals that the melodramatic element is an integral part of the anti-Nazi play. It holds mirror up to a world which is boiling with melodrama. Cruelty and villainy are not figments of the playwright's imagination but stark realities of the existing situation with which the play is concerned. However, as a dramatic artist, Hellman knew that her fiction must do more than demonstrate the strange and awful truth that screamed from the front pages of every daily paper. She, therefore, tried, as Richard Moody notices, "to shift from the massive melodrama of life to the heroic human story of one family behaving like thoroughbreds in an agonizing situation, by making us aware of the blinders we still wore, blinders the European had long since discarded, by alerting us to our own vulnerability."[17] And as Joseph Wood Krutch points out, "such things as Hellman has made the basis of the play do actually go on and that it is not her fault if this is a melodramatic world in which accredited dignitaries of the German Government behave like villains."[18]

A close study of *Watch on the Rhine*, however, reveals that it is not a melodrama, but a Comedy of Manners. American and European characters are thrown together in order to say something about their differing values and customs—not only about good and evil. Mark W. Estrin notes in the play "Hellman's memorably sharp-tongued figures in the person of Fanny Farrelly and the recurrent tone and dialogue of a Jamesian Comedy of Manners."[19] Quantitatively too, there is more comic and romantic by-play in *Watch on the Rhine*, than there is tense melodrama. The children provide some of the comedy in their relationship with their gruff, basically sentimental grandmother. By juxtaposing the warmth between members of the Muller family and the building romance between Marthe and David, Hellman indicates that love will prevail over decadence and hate.

To enhance the dramatic effect further, Hellman introduces blackmail in *Watch on the Rhine* in order to create suspense.

However, the victim of blackmail, Kurt Muller, is not guilty of anything as in *The Children's Hour* and *The Little Foxes*. He is, indeed, more or less admirable in his willingness to behave in such a way as to protect others. Also, the blackmailer, Teck, is different from Mary in *The Children's Hour* as well as from Hubbards in *The Little Foxes*. Teck is an opportunist, thief, and a petty power-seeker. He would like to be a Hubbard but cannot, partly because, like Oscar Hubbard, he lacks the brains, and partly because he has the glimmerings of a conscience and the ability to recognize good when he sees it and differentiate it from evil.

Yet, we may say that blackmail is apparently essential to *Watch on the Rhine*, though, in contrast to the Hubbard plays, more for the sake of theme than plot. If not for Teck's blackmail, nothing else would drive Kurt to murder. And this murder is essential to Hellman's philosophic purpose to show that war and oppression can drive to violence the most philosophically and temperamentally non-violent of men. She also wants to show that not even a wealthy and cultured family on a country estate in a non-combatant country, three thousand miles from war, is safe from war's violence. And also Hellman's view is to show the heroism of the anti-Nazi underground. Except that the murder sends Kurt back to Europe sooner and that too more dangerously the blackmail is necessary to plot in *Watch on the Rhine* only to the extent that it results in the murder of the Count, leaving his wife free to marry the son of the household, David Farrelly. It is also true that the Count might have been a real Nazi who planned to report to the embassy simply out of a sense of duty, without attempting blackmail, but Kurt has a much less ostensible choice, and the necessary point that he chose murder when there seemed to be, from his wife's family's point of view, a viable alternative, would have been lost. Thus, the blackmail forms an integral part of *Watch on the Rhine* and it is not added for the sake of spectacle.

The dramatic effect of the ingenious *Watch on the Rhine* is enhanced also by Hellman's use of metaphors. Properly understood, Teck represents old Europe with its cynical, manipulative, effete aspects which, Hellman believed, made it easy for the fascists to take power. Teck is also a site onto which American audiences can project all their anti-European prejudices, leaving the hero, Kurt, as the New Man of Europe, free for admiration.

The Farrelly living room serves as metaphor for America, in its early nineteenth century origins, its space, its simplicity and above all, in its eclecticism. It is to the credit of Hellman's genius that without even leaving this living room or introducing a single bonafide Nazi into it, she brings home to America the realities of the war and makes the best possible case for our participation in it.

The marriages in *Watch on the Rhine* also serve as metaphors for contrasting models of political relations between the United States and Europe. Marthe's marriage to Teck stands for the aspects of European culture which must be rejected, while Sara's marriage to Kurt stands for those aspects of European culture which must be repatriated into an internationalized version of liberal American ideology. While the childless De-Brancovis marriage represents the depletion, cynicism and amorality, the marriage of Kurt and Sara with its three children, operates as a mediation, a bonding between the best of the old and the new worlds.

A notable feature of *Watch on the Rhine* is that it is free from flat didacticism and sermonizing which are usually evident in thesis plays like Maxwell Anderson's *Key Largo*, Robert Sherwood's *There Shall Be No Night*. Ernest Hemingway's *Fifth Column* and Elmer Rice's *Flight to the West* were prominent in the theatre at the time when *Watch on the Rhine* was staged. It demands greater attention because it deals with the fundamental issue of America of that period with "dignity, insight and sound theatrical intelligence."[20] As a dramatist, Hellman believes in free will and personal responsibility for one's actions or failure to act. Hellman's concern with ethical choices has caused her to study the behaviour of the well-to-do because their money gives them the freedom to make moral choices and to deal with moral responsibilities.

To conclude, it is clear that with *Watch on the Rhine*, Hellman can use Ibsen's methods and strict realism and money as dominant motivation symbol to present a theme of universal significance and power. Viewed solely as a melodrama, solely as the story of Kurt Muller, the play may be dated. But if it is viewed as a story of some naive, liberal Americans put to the test, as call to arms for middle-class Americans, as an exhortation to fight or help those who fight against evil and as character drama like *The Autumn Garden*, then *Watch on the Rhine* still holds validity. It is still charged with meaning and the moral and political questions with which it deals continue to torment us. It is a play of burning intensity for every American who cherishes his life and his country and who believes that human decency could prevail.

NOTES

1. Lillian Hellman, *Watch on the Rhine*, in *The Collected Plays* (Boston, Toronto: Little, Brown, 1971), p. 215.
2. Lillian Hellman, *Pentimento*, cited in Doris V. Falk, *Lillian Hellman* (New York: Frederick Ungar, 1978), p. 67.
3. Rosamind Gilder, "Prizes That Bloom in the Spring," *Theatre Arts Monthly*, 25th June 1941.
4. *Ibid.*
5. Brooks Atkinson, "*Watch on the Rhine*," *The New York Times*, April 2, 1941, p. 26.
6. Basil Wright, "*Watch on the Rhine*," *The Spectator*, 168, May 1, 1942, p. 419.
7. Hellman herself acknowledges this fact in *Pentimento* and her early manuscript drafts of the play. See Doris V. Folk, p. 65.
8. Katherine Lederer, *Lillian Hellman* (Boston: Twayne, 1978), p. 54.
9. Rosamind Gilder, "Prizes That Bloom in the Spring."
10. Barret H. Clark, "Lillian Hellman," *College English*, Vol. 6, No. 3, Dec. 1944, pp. 127-33.
11. Hellman modelled him on a Romanian Prince whom she had met and played poker with him in London in 1936. See Doris V. Falk, p. 66.

12. Barret H. Clark, "Lillian Hellman."
13. Lillian Hellman, *Pentimento: A Book of Portraits* (Boston: Little, Brown, 1973), p. 86.
14. Brooks Atkinson, p. 26.
15. Brendan Gill, "Popular Theatre, *Watch on the Rhine*," *The New Yorker*, Vol. LV, No. 48, Jan. 14, 1980, pp. 55-56.
16. Leonard Ungar, *American Writers Supplement I*, Part I (New York: Charles Scribner's, 1964), p. 279.
17. Richard Moody, *Lillian Hellman: Playwright* (Bobbs-Merrill-Pegasus, 1974), p. 372.
18. Joseph Wood Krutch, "Drama, No Such Animal," *Nation*, Vol. 152, April 12, 1941.
19. Mark W. Estrin, *Critical Essays on Lillian Hellman* (Boston, Mass: G.K. Hall, 1989), p. 12. In *Pentimento*, Hellman herself acknowledges that she is surprised to discover that she had Henry James's two novels on this subject—*The American* and *The Europeans*—in the back of her mind at the time of writing *Watch on the Rhine*.
20. Walcott Gibbs, "That is It," *The New Yorker*, Vol. 17, April 12, 1941, p. 32.

American Indifference to Hitlerism: *The Searching Wind*

The Searching Wind (1944) is an intelligently written play. In a sense, it is an extension of *Watch on the Rhine* which Hellman hoped to follow with a play that would be even more scathing in its denunciation of American indifference to the evils of Hitlerism. In *The Searching Wind*, Hellman advocates anti-fascist activity in an examination of well-meaning, affluent Americans who fail to use their money and influence to halt the progress of Mussolini and Hitler.

The Searching Wind, like *Watch on the Rhine*, sets off the microcosm of manners against the macrocosm of world events. When the two worlds impinged on each other in *Watch on the Rhine*, the liberal upper class Americans were 'shaken out of the magnolias.' In *The Searching Wind*, the magnolias are shaking, but the liberals hardly notice until too late. While *Watch on the Rhine* is a play about action in crisis, *The Searching Wind* is a play about the inaction of bystanders, which is a cardinal sin in Hellman's morality. The inaction takes the form of appeasement and compromises, in love and war, in the private and public world.

The Searching Wind is a structurally intricate play exploring the reasons for the democratic appeasement of fascism in the thirties and human factors which went to make up this social attitude. It is an attempt to analyse the moral failures which had led to war, the liberal equivocations, the self-concerned tolerance for the intolerable. It is Hellman's attempt to establish a connection between private and public morality.

In *The Searching Wind*, Hellman makes a serious comment as she ridicules the previous twenty years of American foreign policy. Instead of portraying Germans succumbing to blood-and-soil rationalism, she displays American diplomats conducting unrequired triangular love affairs during the twenty-year rise of fascism. They are conveniently stationed in key European capitals during 1920-40, and rationalize their failure to request diplomatic censure over Mussolini's Putsch, anti-semitic riots and the annexation of much of central Europe.

The Searching Wind shows rich Americans hopping all over Europe from the year 1922-1944, like Hemingway-type intellectuals in exile. Hellman is really attacking a way of life practised by a minority who made their values—or lack of them—the keynote of their age. The play audits the conduct of an irresolute career diplomat, his retired liberal father-in-law, his bored wife who broke bread with fascist-minded bigwigs.

Set in Washington, D.C., in the spring of 1944, *The Searching Wind* deals with the family of an American diplomat, Alexander Hazen, an attache at Rome, during the rise of Mussolini and Hitler. A 'liberal,' Alexander Hazen turns out to be one who cannot believe in villainy, and who in the name of caution, and keeping an open mind, made compromises with evil—with fascism, at the cost of lives of future generations. Three scenes take place in the present—1944—the year in which the action begins and ends. And Hellman reviews the rise of fascism and the triumph of appeasement in three flashbacks. These three flashback scenes take place in 1922, 1923 and 1938 respectively. The flashback scenes also represent three personal crises in the lives of the three major characters—Alexander Hazen, a career diplomat, his wealthy wife, Emily Hazen and the 'other woman,' Cassie Bowman. At each political crisis, Alex appeases the fascists, and his wife appeases her rival—her ex-best friend, Cassie. Alex tries to appease both the women. Outside the trio, as commentators on the action, are the old man, Moses Taney, Emily's father, and the young man, Sam Hazen, Emily and Alexander Hazen's son.

The framework of present time opens and closes with the conflict between Emily and Cassie. Hellman creates both curiosity and befuddlement in her audience by having Emily invite Cassie to hers and Alex's home in Washington—nobody knows why. Then, through the subsequent flashbacks into the past, until in the final scene, at the house, a few hours after scene one, we learn Emily's purpose. Hellman presents the past as a series of double crisis confrontations.

In the 1922 scene, Moses Taney, his daughter, Emily, and her best friend, Cassie, along with Taney's maid, Sophronia are visiting Rome, where Alex Hazen is a young diplomat in the American embassy. Mussolini is marching on Rome and Cassie is marching on Alex, whom Emily expects to marry. Mussolini takes over. Alex agrees with his boss, the American ambassador, that open opposition to the fascists would be intervention in Italian internal affairs. His failure to take a strong political stand precipitates a quarrel with Cassie. This is not known to Emily that Alex and Cassie are lovers and have thought of marriage. Now Cassie decides to return to her teaching job in America for a year to think it over. Emily's response to Cassie and her challenge is that of passive resistance—to stay in Rome where Alex is. It works, and Cassie catches him.

The second political scene is in Berlin in 1923. It is the time of the first organized anti-semitic riots. Emily is married to Alex and Cassie has made it a habit to follow them and meet Alex, when she is on vacation in Europe. The scene takes place in a Berlin restaurant where Alex is waiting for Emily and unknowingly being watched by Cassie at another table. The noises of riot and threats against Jews are heard outside the restaurant. Emily comes in shocked by the spectacle she has just witnessed of German ex-soldiers beating up old Jews. Alex's response to the crisis is to calm down the people in the restaurant and to blame the riot on the negligence of the police. He refuses to face the complicity of the police in the anti-semitism. On the other hand, Emily sees Cassie and is polite. Cassie takes the offensive and accuses Emily of having stolen Alex from her. Emily claims not guilty—Cassie and Alex had already quarrelled. Emily offers friendship, reconciliation and appeasement.

The third double confrontation takes place in Paris in 1938 when the Munich agreement—the arch example of appeasement of Hitler by Britain and France—is about to take place. Alex must send his recommendation to the United States Government. Again, he refuses to believe in evil and corruption, even when a Nazi attempts to pressurize him into trying to keep France and Britain out of war with Germany. He holds out hope that Hitler may keep his promise not to annex more territory after the Sudetenland, and supports Chamberlain's efforts to keep 'peace in our time.'

Emily also wants peace at any price, now in politics as well as love. She does not want to send her son to war. She and Alex quarrel—then make peace—about her hob-nobbing with pro-Nazi European socialites, including the banker with whom she has deposited some of her money.

But Cassie, at Emily's invitation, has been to see Alex. Before Emily arrives, they have arranged a rendezvous. Alex has decided that he loves Emily but is 'in love with' Cassie. When Emily comes, she tells Alex that as she entered she saw Cassie in the lobby but was afraid to confront her. And thus, she leaves Alex in the hands of the enemy, as Chamberlain—and Alex—left Europe.

In the last scene, which takes up the 1944 action again, Hellman brings all the confrontations together—the women, the war, the generations. It turns out that Emily had invited Cassie to the house in act one in order to have it out with her once and for all to accuse her directly of husband-stealing. Now Cassie breaks down and tells Emily that the accusation is true. She had been out to get Alex away from Emily and to punish Emily for marrying him. Alex agrees to let Cassie go without a struggle, and he relaxes with his wife.

The major confrontation, however, is between Sam Hazen and his elders. This, too, has been hanging fire since the opening scene. We learned there that Sam had been wounded. Now we find that he must lose his leg. In spite of his grandfather's efforts to educate him, Sam is not an intellectual—he trusts action and sincere human relations, not words. He had felt at home in the army with fighting men, and especially with his friend, Leck, who was killed in the same battle in which Sam was wounded. His war experiences have made him ashamed of his family of 'bystanders' and now he tells them why.

Sam is ashamed of his grandfather, the great liberal, who now just sits back and watches. He is also ashamed of his father who went along with Munich, and of his mother with her rich, pro-Nazi friends. Then, with an almost apologetic patriotism, Sam accuses his parents of damaging the country which he loves. He harshly tells them: I don't want any more of Father's mistakes, for any reason, good or bad, or yours, Mother, because I think they do [the country] harm. . . . I am ashamed of both of you, and that's the truth."[1]

The play ends with Samuel denouncing his parents and their generation for bringing on the war by closing their eyes to what was happening and for feeling ashamed to express their love of country at a time when such an expression was necessary. In this sense, the play is reminiscent of *Days to Come*, making the point clear that the world is the sum total of each person's personal actions. Thus, *The Searching Wind* is not a formal play, though it is concerned with a profound truth. There is no true villain in the play. The only villain seems to be appeasement of people. All the major characters just let things happen, stand around and watch the earth and the people on it being eaten. And, as Lederer observes, "a searching wind blows away the rationalizations of all the characters by the end of the play, as they learn the truth about themselves."[2]

The Searching Wind is notable for its novel plot with its multiple-scene scheme, bringing some film techniques to bear upon its structural unity. Although Hellman never held the movie industry in high esteem, she learned its techniques well enough to use them in her most ambitious play, *The Searching Wind*. Told through flashbacks, *The Searching Wind* is the kind of play that puts great demands on the cast. Act I moves from 1944 to 1922 and back to 1944. Act II moves from 1923 to 1938 and full circle to 1944. The first two acts, showing the onset of fascism in Rome and Berlin, are well done, though both are cluttered by the development of the love triangle. The third flashback is notable for a delineation of the Nazi diplomat who deals with the Munich pact.

However, many critics contend that the multiple scenes and numerous major characters in the play divert the audiences from Hellman's thematic intentions, thereby marring its structural unity. For instance, Richard Moody says: "the segmented structure is loose as a haystack and also reduced the firepower of the political message. It might have held on longer performances, if she had not tried so hard to write two plays at once, one political, the other personal."[3] Casper H. Nannee feels: "*The Searching Wind* has two centers around which the plot revolves. One is the willingness of American businessmen to do business with Hitler and Mussolini and the other is the pent-up feelings of returned soldiers towards those who brought on the war by closing their eyes to what was going on."[4] The *Time* reviewer points out that *The Searching Wind* is "more like two plays—and two very unequal ones."[5] Doris V. Falk says: "neither the theme, nor the plot structure, nor the characters ever came completely clear on the stage—and they take considerable analyzing even on the printed page."[6] And Katherine Lederer writes: "the attempt to tell two stories at once makes the impact of the play diffuse, although the theme is clear enough."[7] Downer contends: "Hellman was so caught up in contemporary issues that the structure of the drama is faulty."[8]

Thus, critics feel that the structural beauty of the play is spoiled chiefly because of the simultaneous treatment of two divergent stories within the scope of a single plot as in the case of *The Children's Hour*. The critics seem to have taken a cue from T.S. Eliot's critical pronouncement on Shakespeare's *Hamlet* that the play is a film on which two photographs have been taken.

But a deeper understanding of the play reveals that Hellman has done an admirable job in solving the technical difficulties arising from resolving the personal problem by way of merging it into worldly problems. It is not fair to stress the parallel too strongly as some critics have actually done. For, it is to be borne in mind that the story is dramatised in terms of 'surface realism' and any attempt to find *raison d'etre* would destroy the needed illusion. As Barret H. Clark explains, "the author, having established on a solid dramatic basis, the personal drama, a drama in itself complete—resists the temptation to point out that what was wrong with individuals is precisely what is wrong with the nations."[9] Furthermore, as Sievers observes, "if there is a weakness in *The Searching Wind*, it is that the plot construction is not of the tense cat-and-mouse battle of minds that made Hellman's Hubbard plays memorable. Charmingly weak characters are more difficult to deal with dramatically than wilfully sadistic ones."[10]

Like the plot-construction, Hellman's art of characterization in *The Searching Wind* is met with certain criticism. For instance, Richard Moody thinks that the characters "appear banal and inconsequential. Nor do the characters assume any stature. With the possible exception of Moses Taney, the portraits are little more than line drawings."[11]

But, a close study of the play reveals that Hellman's characters in *The Searching Wind* are more vulnerable than the superhuman characters in *Watch on the Rhine* because of their patriotic fervour. We should also remember that in *The Searching Wind* Hellman has painted her characters on a historical canvas. On top of that she seeks to convey the helplessness of individuals in responsible positions when they cannot take their own stand. She also creates a microcosm-macrocosm relationship between the trio—Alexander Hazen, Emily Hazen and Cassie Bowman—and their times. The compromises that Alex, Emily and Cassie made in their own lives are repeated on an international scale. Alex becomes an ambassador, thereby choosing a life of appeasement. In Emily, he finds the ideal ambassador's wife—apolitical and affluent. Cassie bemoans her generation: "We are an ignorant generation." (333) Yet, she spends her summers in Europe to be near Alex whose weakness she condemns but whose company she needs. Even in 1933, as Jews are being harassed in the streets of Berlin, Cassie and Emily enjoy the security of a cafe where they argue about Alex.

Within the limits of communist rationalizing, Hellman successfully depicts the individuals who are most to be blamed for the unchecked development of fascism. They are people who have outlived an epoch and cannot shake loose from passivity to act effectively either for their own happiness or the national good. And, apart from their politics, they most resemble the figures of Hellman's 'Chekhovian' plays—*The Autumn Garden* and *Toys in the Attic*.

Coming to individual characters, Alexander Hazen, the hero of the two ladies, Emily Hazen and Cassie Bowman, may also be said to be the hero of *The Searching Wind*. He is portrayed as a sincere idealist. As Cassie remarks, he is a man "who didn't know what he was doing." (297) He is an American diplomat, an attache in Rome, who follows an isolationist policy during the rise of Mussolini and Hitler in order to escape from the ugly truth. His political philosophy is a carry-over from his unresolved emotional life.

Alex's life is one of compromise and rationalizing, in spite of his basic good nature and idealism. The pattern extends from his betrayal of Cassie and marrying of Emily to his career as a diplomat. In his political career, he contributes significantly to the American policy of appeasement which reached its climax at the time of the Munich Conference in 1938.

Watching as he does fascism become real, bold and imperious, Alex is at once a decent and a muddled man. Though he is dismayed by what he sees, he hangs on to the hope that somehow good will come of evil. As his stake is in the status quo, he instinctively makes out a case for appeasement. Despite his now clearer view of what is happening, and despite his aroused conscience, he sends a report back to his government offering equivocal support for appeasement. He defends himself against his conscience by insisting that the individual cannot hope to deflect the course of history. It is his belief that the protest of the individual is useless that makes him so weak.

Despite the accumulating evidence of crisis, Alexander remains convinced that things are not as bad as they seem. Cast as a stereotype of Woodrow Wilson, Hazen refuses to see the threat in Mussolini's rise. He tries to rationalize it. Regarding the Nazi evil and the threat of war, he is befuddled and confused. The developments in Europe are 'strange' to him and he does not know what is best for him. Thus Alex remains one of the most complex characters of Hellman. He is a figure of no real power himself. Yet, he remains the spokesman for the official blunders, delays and defections that made Munich no terminus.

The next important and interesting character in *The Searching Wind* is Cassie Bowman who is the lover of Alexander Hazen. She is intelligent and idealistic in her insistence that Alex should take a firm stand. Though John Gassner calls her "high minded,"[12] her actions are certainly not high-minded.

It is to be noted that Cassie has more life and she is more assertive than Emily and Alexander. Hers is the most forceful dialogue. In Rome, she says to Alex: "A revolution is going on out there. But by this time next year it will be nothing more than dinner table conversation. Things mean so little to us, to you." (304) She says to Emily: "Do stop playing the piano. It doesn't go well with guns." (304) Cassie appears to be Hellman's spokesman. It is Cassie, who at the end of the play, explains to herself and the others what they have done with their lives: "I don't want to see another generation of people like us, who didn't know what they were doing or why they did it. . . . We were frivolous people." (333)

Moses Taney is yet another interesting character in the play. He provides philosophical comment on the action like a chorus in Greek drama. He is a charming but disillusioned fighting liberal, retired editor of a once great newspaper. He has cynically abandoned his fighting newspaper and has withdrawn himself from political decision-making, but comments bitterly on other people's diplomatic compromises. He closely parallels the wise old man, Joshuva Farrelly, of *Watch on the Rhine*. He points out Alex's mistake by giving his view: "that bad men are stupid and good men are smart." (290) But, this 'scornful old liberal,' who knows better the circumstances that led to war, himself behaves worse.

However, the most fascinating character in *The Searching Wind* is Sam Hazen, son of Alexander and Emily Hazen. He is of a younger generation and speaks for the author as Julie does in *Days to Come* and the youngsters in *Watch on the Rhine*. Hellman obviously intended Sam to show us that the sins of the fathers are visited on the children. Sam was in the army and he saw history taking shape for which he was not responsible in any way, though as an army man he was also taking part in it. He vehemently questions the stance taken by his parents and his grandfather as by-standers without making an attempt to change the course of history. He was proud of his parents until one day when his fellow army man gives a newspaper cutting which says that many of the self-proclaimed righteous people including his parents had business dealings with Germany.

Like Alexandra in *The Little Foxes*, Sam is bitter about his father, because he is an appeaser. With the full truth spread out for the first time before him, he cries shame upon the parents he loves. What is more, he demands passionately that there are no such mistakes again for any reason. Sam is the heir to the mistakes of his predecessors, that is, his parents and grandparents, who have caused him to fight in war and to lose a leg in the process. He urges his parents:

> I don't want any more of my father's mistakes. . . . I am ashamed of you both, and that's the truth. I don't want to be ashamed that way again. I don't like losing my leg. . . . I'm scared—but everybody's welcome to it as long as it means a little something and helps to bring us out some place. (337)

Sam knows that "history is made by the masses of people" (334) not by one or two men and he can only hope that the loss of a leg will make people less frivolous. Thus, Sam is one of Hellman's soldier-boys, who has finally found a purposeful life in the army.

Emily Hazen, the wife of Alexander Hazen, is a one-time best friend of Cassie Bowman. Emily uses her power tactics to win Alexander from Cassie and marries him. She is a woman who derives her pleasure from consorting with those very businessmen and politicians who had facilitated the rise of the forces which eventually wound her own son. Emily, throughout the play, strives to learn how Cassie feels and in what way Cassie's affair with her husband reflects all three participants in the situation. And at one point she stresses the need for getting things straight, but all that she says is: "We've started it; let's finish it. . . . It's time to find out." (333) Thus, Emily Hazen too, like Alexander Hazen, is an appeaser, but in her case, she forgives Cassie all through the play.

The Searching Wind is important for its intense realism. Like *Watch on the Rhine*, it is contemporary in its content. The play is set at crucial moments in the history of the rise of fascism: in Rome, in 1922, at the time of Mussolini's take-over in Italy; in Berlin, in 1923, as the first signs of Hitler's rise becomes apparent; in Paris, on the eve of Chamberlain's appeasement. Hellman herself told in an interview:

> Like every other writer. I use myself and the time I live in. The nearest things to a political play was *The Searching Wind*. . . . I meant only to write about nice, well-born people who, with good intentions, helped to sell out a world.[13]

The Searching Wind, even more than *Watch on the Rhine*, derives its strength from its immediacy. In the words of Richard Moody, "With Eisenhower's invasion of France two months away, with the Nazis still threatening we struggled to know where we went wrong in bringing the civilized world to the edge of disaster."[14] The 1920s were a time of debased epicureanism. When it came time for history to test the convictions of the 1920s, it turned out that there were none. The endless parties in *The Searching Wind* are spin-offs of Jay Gatsby's extravaganzas where it made no difference who attended. Such a lack of discrimination may have been acceptable then. But the careless men of the 1920s spilled over into the next decade when frivolous Emilies sat next to Nazis and fascists at soirees, making small talk and never challenging their political beliefs for fear of a breach of etiquette.

With keen awareness of the interaction of psychological and political factors, Lillian Hellman shows the isolationist foreign policy during the thirties as an inevitable expression of the personal escapism of the men who made the policy. As Barret Clark observes, "there is the heart of the problem, Miss Hellman has sought to elucidate, if not to solve."[15]

Hellman's attitude to the contemporary political situation is quite clear. The innocent Americans in *The Searching Wind* win admiration for their simple charm and carefree attitudes. But their ignorance of evil and poverty, their lack of concern for the disturbing events between the wars and their efforts to be nice guys constitute a flawed existence. Innocence is not enough. In the context of twentieth century political developments, it is actually a liability. As N.S. Pradhan observes, "written under the shadow of war, *The Searching Wind* contains the denunciation of a so-called innocence which makes the American look like a fool in the eyes of the world."[16]

The Searching Wind is not only intensely realistic but also extremely satirical. The play is a scathing indictment of a generation of smug American indifference to Hitlerism. The ultimate power of the play rests with the bitter-sad indictment of the appeasers and with the documentary reminder of Munich. It satirises the passive complacency of the generation that could sit idly by and witness the persecution of an entire group of people without active protest.

The ever-seeking playwright, Hellman, is not content with spinning a little fable and tacking an appendix onto it. And so, she conceived a dramatic structure which combines a personal knot of conflicting wills with a roughly parallel knot showing how a world-wide situation is only an amplified personal drama on a large scale. Hellman herself emphasized this in an interview:

> there were not only a lot of bastards who fixed things up in the last 10 or 12 years, but nice people, too, (as in their personal lives) can do bad things from the right motives. I know I don't start by telling myself to write a play about War. What War, whose War? What occurs to me first are the people.[17]

Hellman employs dramatic irony in *The Searching Wind*, but not as thoroughly as in her earlier plays. We know before the characters do that Sam must lose his leg. We know before Emily that Alex and Cassie have an affair and physical relation. But the organization of the play is such that we learn much of the information along with the characters. Strangely enough, Emily, the detective,' who instigates the search for the truth in their lives, never explains why she wants to know it in 1944, what she has not faced in previous twenty years. We get the best explanation in Emily's words to Alex: "But there's a great deal that you don't know, and Cassie doesn't know, and I don't either. It's time to find out." (333)

Hellman also employs 'boomerang irony' in *The Searching Wind.* Alexander went to World War I because no one acted to prevent that war. He feels that his father's description of France did not match with what he saw at first hand. Sam feels that the Italy he fought in does not fit the Italy Alexander describes. And Sam goes to war, of course, because his father's generation let it happen. Cassie, by quarrelling with Alex, loses the chance to influence him to take a definite moral stand. Emily, who influenced Alex to support appeasement because she did not want Sam to go to war, is then indirectly the cause of his being wounded. Like the dowager in *Watch on the Rhine* and the matriarch to come in *The Autumn Garden*, Moses makes ironic comments throughout the play, but he is as guilty as the rest, having abdicated a position of power and responsibility from which his viewpoint might have had some influence.

The Searching Wind is not without its symbolic significance. The very title of the play is symbolic. Hellman told an interviewer that she had got the title from a Negro maid:

> Some mornings when she came she'd say 'it's a searching wind today.' She meant one of those winds that go right through you to your backbone. I suppose in my title I was thinking of the wind that's blowing through the world.[18]

The author's own explanation of the title, however, makes the play more meaningful. In her memoir, *An Unfinished Woman*,

Hellman says: "It takes a searching wind to find the tree you sit in who can tell what side you are on if you don't know your own mind?"[19] In the memoir, this sentence is applied to upper class liberal attitudes towards racism.

To conclude, *The Searching Wind* is a highly provocative play of the season. Unlike Hellman's other great plays—*The Children's Hour, The Little Foxes*, and *Watch on the Rhine—The Searching Wind* is not predominantly taut and intense. Its span is long and its world spacious. Hellman has pitched a handful of lives into the swirling history of our age. It also delves into the psyche of the young generation which has the moral responsibility, for the sake of humanity, to put all the splintered pieces of the West and rebuild a more humane civilization. They are not responsible for the disaster and yet they have the task of redeeming the situation.

Hellman's treatment of the liberal crisis is interesting since, despite many setbacks, she never questions the validity of her liberal views. The liberal characters remain shattered, but, at the same time, Hellman also creates other personal situations to make the play more effective. Although the play points to certain social circumstances of a particular stage in history, the universal situation makes *The Searcing Wind* timeless in its treatment of the human predicament.

NOTES

1. Lillian Hellman, *The Searching Wind*, in *The Collected Plays* (Boston-Toronto: Little, Brown, 1971), p. 337.
2. Katherine Lederer, *Lillian Hellman* (Boston: Twayne, 1979), p. 60.
3. Richard Moody, *Lillian Hellman: Playwright* (New York: Bobbs-Merrill, 1972), pp. 156-57.
4. Casper H. Nannee, "Nazism and Fascism," *Politics in the American Drama* (Boston: Twayne, 1960), pp. 142-43.
5. "New Plays in Manhattan," *Time*, Vol. 43, April 24, 1944, p. 72.
6. Doris V. Falk, *Lillian Hellman* (New York: Frederick Ungar, 1978), p. 75.

7. Katherine Lederer, p. 60.
8. Alan S. Downer, *Fifty Years of American Drama: 1900-1950* (New York: Henry Regnery, 1951), p. 61.
9. Barret H. Clark, "Lillian Hellman," *College English*, Vol. 6, Dec. 1944, No. 3, p. 133.
10. David Sievers, "A History of Psychoanalysis and the American Drama," *Freud on Broadway* (New York: Hermitage, 1955), p. 287.
11. Richard Moody, p. 156.
12. John Gassner, "Entropy in the Drama," *Theatre Arts*, 35, September 1951, pp. 16-17.
13. Lillian Hellman, Winter 132, cited in Katherine Lederer, p. 65.
14. Richard Moody, pp. 155-56.
15. Barret H. Clark, p. 133.
16. N.S. Pradhan, "Innocence," *Modern American Drama: A Study in Myth and Tradition*, p. 38.
17. Lillian Hellman, *Post Man*, March 12, 1944.
18. Lillian Hellman, *Herald Tribune*, April 9, 1944.
19. Lillian Hellman, *An Unfinished Woman* (Boston: Little, Brown, 1969), p. 12.

Destructive Postures of the Jungle-creatures: *Another Part of the Forest*

In *Another Part of the Forest* (1946), Hellman returns to the milieu of the Hubbard family twenty years prior to the action of *The Little Foxes* (1938) to trace the origins of the villainy and greed that destroyed their lives. It may well be called the prologue to the first play. Hellman's aim is to look into their family background and to find out what it was that made them the nasty people they were. The play chronicles the life of the Hubbards in 1880 prior to their 'little foxes' incarnation. It reveals a harsher world with greater animal death-grips and destructive postures of the jungle-creatures.

Naturally, Hellman lays great emphasis on the social ostracizing of the Hubbards and their impulse to get ahead financially to compensate for their loneliness. Even twenty years of time does not transport them to the age of innocence inasmuch as their evil natures are already well-cultivated. Although the play has its own independent life, it is remarkably enhanced by our fore-knowledge of the despicable and fascinating Hubbards. It is more analytic and less concentrated in the picture of evil.

In *Another Part of the Forest*, we see the beginnings of the family's internal struggle for power and domination, a struggle which is meant to particularise the ruthless economic power and domination which they wield over their community. The Hubbards are grasping vicious predators feeding off the 'Reconstruction South' as they claw their way upward. They come to us essentially as merchants in a broken agricultural economy. It reveals not only the dubious ways in which the Hubbards accumulated their wealth but also the ways in which women function as commodities.

The play centres on the family patriarch, Marcus Hubbard, a

self-made man who becomes rich during the civil war by charging outrageous sums for necessities. His sons, Ben and Oscar and his daughter, Regina, play the same game of grabbing and backstabbing as they do in *The Little Foxes*. All the same, there is a heightened level of sadism and acquisitiveness all around. It emphasizes Hellman's theme that not only are the sins of the father passed on to the sons, but the capacity for sinning as well.

Another Part of the Forest may be said to be a Marxian study of the decline of the Southern feudal aristocracy and the rise of the capitalist exploiter. The play is concerned with materialism, amorality and the New South in two periods of time. Despite Hellman's obvious concern with social evil, here she seems to be preoccupied with abstract evil, even to the point of caricature.

Set in June 1880, in Alabama, *Another Part of the Forest* delves deep into the imaginary past to unearth the psychological factors that made Regina and her brothers the predatory creatures they became as a result of their father's sadistic, driving ambition for wealth and power. The saga of the Hubbards begins with Marcus Hubbard, the father, a tyrannical manipulator of his entire family. He made a fortune through illegal commerce during the Civil War and is now replacing the aristocratic Bagtry clan as the chief force in the region. His family, however, provides little assistance to his ambitions. Marcus's wife, Lavinia Hubbard, is weak-minded and preoccupied with religion. Ben the eldest son and heir is a rebellious and ambitious enemy who opposes him at every turn. The second son, Oscar Hubbard, is half-witted and has fallen into a vulgar love with a prostitute, Laurette Sincee. His daughter, Regina, is conducting a secret affair with John Bagtry of the aristocratic family. Regina has displaced her mother, Lavinia, in her father's affections and father's attachment to his daughter is given incestuous overtones and there is more than a hint that Ben is a jealous rival of his father for Regina, as well as for his money. However, the entire town despises them and they have become pariahs in their own town.

In contrast to the Hubbards are the Bagtrys—Birdie, her mother, and her cousin, John Bagtry. They are the 'land and cotton poor,' starving on their plantation, Lionnet. And because of their aristocratic heritage and manners, they are a thorn in the side of the Hubbards. Marcus, encouraged by Ben, plans to gain control of the Bagtry plantation through secretly lending money to the daughter of the family—the childish and light-headed Birdie Bagtry. He leaves the affair in the hands of Ben, who tries to trick him by pretending that the loan is for ten thousand dollars, but keeping five thousand dollars for himself. Oscar too is involved in this cheating as he wants money to go to New Orleans with the local whore, Laurette.

Ben invites Birdie and John Bagtry to his father's 'musicale' and also makes Oscar invite his love, Laurette. Ben, who is always jealous of his father's love to Regina wants to thwart Regina's desire of marrying John Bagtry. And he also plans to get his father enraged at Oscar for his affair with the prostitute. In return, Regina exposes Ben's finagling. When Marcus discovers the deception, a fierce struggle breaks out between father and son. Marcus orders Ben to leave the house.

In the third act, Ben bids his mother, Lavinia, goodbye as he is going to leave the house as per his father's orders. At this point, Lavinia babbles Ben to take her with him, as she always wants to go away and start a school for black children. She has persuaded her husband, Marcus, for starting this school but Marcus has paid no heed. Lavinia also reveals to Ben that she knows a secret that is dangerous to Marcus.

Ben is reluctant until his mother gradually gives him the information about his father's past that could hang Marcus if it became known in the town. The townspeople already hate him for exploiting them during the Civil War, by selling the badly needed salt, smuggled through the blockade, for extraordinary black-market prices. Moreover, the townspeople have suspected that he led the Union troops to a camp where Southern boys—sons and brothers of the local folks—were training and where the Yankees slaughtered twenty-seven boys, including John Bagtry's twin. Marcus has always had an alibi to protect him from the charge, but Lavinia has the proof that his alibi is false. It is written in her Bible, along with her own and Coralee's eyewitness account of Marcus's whereabouts on the night of the massacre. Ben coaxes it from her and in exchange promises to finance her school and take care of Coralee, the black servant.

Armed with this knowledge, Ben becomes the tribal chief. He forces his father to escape hanging, to sell him the family business for one dollar. He gives Birdie Bagtry a promised loan on Lionnet and insures that the plantation will come eventually to the Hubbards by clearing the way for Oscar to court Birdie. John Bagtry is out of the way too, for the money will enable him to go to Brazil, his long cherished wish. Ruling his family with an iron hand, he marries Regina to Horace Giddens, a young clerk who lives in Mobile, and is thus far away enough not to have heard the scandal of her affair with John.

In the final moments of the play, Marcus, now stripped of power, goes to sit by his daughter, but she ignores him and crosses to a chair near Ben. As the curtain comes down, Regina, now knowing where her bread is buttered, acknowledges Ben's superiority. Thus, in one terrifying act, the later destinies of this family of foxes are determined and the sequel now seems to stand out in bold illumination.

Thus, Hellman, with her psychoanalytic perception, succeeds brilliantly in showing that evil begets evil through family dynamics—the influence of parents upon children and the creation of pressures within the family that required outside release. There is a kind of malevolent magnificence in the scenes in which brother, sister and father pit their wits and unbridled aggression against one another devoid of humanity or affection.

Another Part of the Forest, like *The Little Foxes*, is known for its tight plot-construction, leading to a violent climax that is the result of evil doing. But, unlike the other plays of Hellman, *Another Part of the Forest* is the only 'end play' in Hellman's canon. Here Hellman introduces two strong individual portraitures—Marcus and Lavinia—who are the parents of Ben, Oscar and Regina. But, as the play progresses, these two are dropped out of the main conflict. As in *The Little Foxes*, the conflict between Regina and Ben forms the main action of the play. So the structure of the play is not concerned, as Bigsby observes, "with uncovering a set of experiences or perceptions which could explain their character and their actions but simply with exposing a hidden part which can be utilised to shift the balance of power."[1]

Suspense is built powerfully till Lavinia's final revelation of a piece of suppressed information in the last act. This piece of hidden information becomes a central part of the play's dramatic strategy and is hinted at throughout and then flourished at a critical moment. Again, as in *The Little Foxes*, the crucial reversal centres around a character's learning a piece of information which can be used as "a lever against the rest of the family in this never-ending competition for superiority."[2]

Thus, the climax of the play and the defeat of Marcus is brought about by Lavinia, his downtrodden wife. The audience has the pleasure, rare in a Hellman play, of watching virtue triumph or at least find its own reward. By the end of the last scene, the later action of the plundering 'little foxes' appears inevitable, illuminated by the lightning flash into their past.

Another Part of the Forest is remarkable not only for its tight plot-construction but also for its superb characterization. The characters in *Another Part of the Forest* easily surpass those of *The Little Foxes* in their vicious treatment of one another. And, as Joseph Wood Krutch notes, "by comparison the first play would have to be ranked as an idyll."[3] As in *The Little Foxes*, Hellman is uninterested in drawing sympathetic characters or generous human emotions, and presents "sharply etched characters who fascinate in their malignancy."[4]

Among the Hubbards—Marcus Hubbard, Ben Hubbard, Oscar Hubbard, Lavinia Hubbard and Regina Hubbard—Marcus, Ben and Regina are vigorous and unforgettable characters. Marcus, who is the father and head of this Hubbard clan, is a self-made man who got his smuggling started during the Civil War. During the war, he inadvertently led Union troops to an encampment of local boys, who were killed. He ostracized Alabama townspeople and started dominating the town. Cruel, cold-blooded with a sardonic wit and a partly pretentious feeling for culture, he cares only, and then half-incestuously, for his daughter, Regina. Disappointed in his sons, Marcus placed in Regina his hopes for someone to share his love for culture. Marcus scorns and ridicules his wife, Lavinia, and becomes Oscar's model for his treatment of Birdie in *The Little Foxes*. His treatment of his wife along with her knowledge of his guilty past has made her a violent hysteric. His contempt for his sons, the power-craving son Ben and the spineless Oscar, has made them bitterly hostile.

The sins of which Marcus stands convicted include greed, avarice, false pride, false witness, lack of love and incestuous desire, presumably unfulfilled. Like Faulkner's Thomas Sutpen, Marcus wants to found a dynasty. But he laments the wicked offspring fate has given him. But he deserves no better. He is a sadist. The big fox could not have had a family of anything but 'little foxes.' His downfall is the downfall of an ignoble man. His retribution comes, at the hands of his own family, not surprisingly, given Hellman's attitude to evil and the framework of the Greek tragedy which she has chosen for pattern.

Thus, in Marcus, Hellman creates what many critics regarded as her most interesting character. A prototype of all the iron-willed tyrants in Tennessee Williams' plays, Marcus is more complicated. He despises his sons and his feeling for Regina is his downfall. Marcus is right when he describes himself as "an empty man from an idiot world. A man who believes in nothing and never will. A man in space!"[5]

Ben Hubbard, the elder son of Marcus, is the most interesting of the Hubbard progeny. He is the outcome of his father's ruthlessness, the fulfilment of his father's spirit. Hellman, as in *The Little Foxes*, again depicts Ben as a role-player, literally a hypocrite. In *Another Part of the Forest*, Ben is interested only in money and the power it brings and he has every reason to hate his father. When he gains the upper hand, he says to Marcus: "Don't waste your time, or put yourself in further danger, or tempt me longer. Ever since you started your peculiar way of treating me, many years ago, I have had ugly dreams." (412)

With no concrete passions to cloud his judgement, Ben watches and waits for the others to make mistakes. He can even be sardonic about being unloved. At the end of the play, Ben usurps power from his father, Marcus, and becomes a tyrannical chief of his family. In his ambition and ruthlessness, Ben thus proves himself equal to Marcus.

Regina Hubbard, the sister of Ben and daughter of Marcus, is the most interesting woman character in the entire Hubbard family. Hellman portrays Regina as a coquettish girl of twenty. She is in love and has an affair with the penniless John Bagtry at the beginning of the play. She hopes to get him to elope with her to Chicago, since she knows that neither her father nor Ben would even approve their marriage.

Regina is crafty and scheming. Although she is aware of her father's incestuous attraction to her, she is perfectly willing to use her feminine charms to persuade him to grant her wishes. She plays the role of ladylike subservience to gain some advantage for herself and longs fiercely for the same power, which Ben, her brother, attains.

But, Regina is no match to Ben, because she still wants something human—love. Although she assumes a mask with Marcus, she is fairly straightforward with Ben. Though Regina is as powerless as her mother, Lavinia, and Birdie, she does not acquiesce. Instead, she uses the methods that she has seen the men employ. She plays her father and Ben off against each other, informing Ben about Marcus and Marcus about Ben so that she may gain the confidence of both. She becomes rock hard yet extraordinarily vital, a combination of cool villainy and hot desire that is developed in *The Little Foxes* into one of the most commanding and repellent female characters on the American stage.

Though at times Hellman's characterization of women may appear harsh, she affords her audience the opportunity to explore the conditions of a woman's life which may lead to manipulating, possessive and emasculating behaviour. As Hellman probes the background of Regina's character, she finds a lonely girlhood at least partly the cause of her later rapacity. No wonder, the Regina of twenty years later knows only ruthlessness. She has suffered from a feeling of aloofness since childhood days and has known nothing to make her appreciate the warmth of human affection. Thus her coup in *The Little Foxes* may be seen as the culmination of many years of having had to claw her way to the inner circle. She is "a woman in a seething microcosm of a man's world the dynasty of Marcus Hubbard."[6] Hence to despise Regina is to despise a typhoon.

Oscar Hubbard is the last character to be mentioned in the vicious Hubbard clan. Oscar is shown as a pathetic weakling in love with a prostitute, Laurette Sincee, on the pattern of Freud's comment on 'love for a harlot.' Oscar is simple-minded. He is deeply and sincerely in love with the town-whore and wants to marry her and take her to New Orleans. He reminds us of his son, Leo, in *The Little Foxes*, when he emerges onto the porch stuffing a biscuit in his mouth. He too, is forced by Ben to marry Birdie at the end of the play.

Lavinia, the down-trodden wife of Marcus Hubbard, lives, like Birdie of *The Little Foxes*, according to the dictates of men. She is unlike her children. Though broken and half-crazed from living with a man who shows only contempt for her, she is a good woman, deeply religious in a child-like sense. Hellman describes Lavinia as a "woman of about forty eight, stooped, thin, delicate looking." (346) Lavinia's character is modelled on Hellman's mother who was a sweet eccentric.[7]

Lavinia, like Glaspell's Minnie Wright of *Trifles*, fears the brutality of her husband. Her actions are governed first by her husband, Marcus, and then by her son, Ben. Marcus scorns and ridicules her whereas her children treat her with complete contempt. Lavinia, who lacks both intellect and education, is a mass of confused guilt and is nearly insane. She always lives in a dark world of her own without any sunshine or light. As she tells Coralee she "spent a life afraid." (366)

Though Lavinia and Coralee share the secret of her husband's sin, Lavinia keeps it to herself till the climax of the play. Out of her overwhelming sense of guilt which makes her almost mad, she turns to religion for peace of mind. She recognises the culpability of Marcus which, she feels, has brought a curse upon her family, and wishes to take some responsibility for it. She says: "I got to do a little humble service. I lived in sin these thirty seven years." (367)

Though Lavinia is portrayed as a neurotic woman, she is a woman of principle under all her submissiveness. She knows well that her marriage is on the brink of collapse and tries her best to keep it from falling by being a devoted wife. When Marcus threatens to send her away to a mental hospital, Lavinia makes up her mind to escape. Lavinia is at last free and happy. With a beaming face, she tells her family: "I'll be thinking of you and I'll be praying for you, all of you. Everybody needs somebody to pray for them, and I'm going to pray for you all." (421) To each of the Hubbards, she gives a memento—a pin to Regina, her prayer book to Oscar, her father's watch to Ben, and her wedding ring back to Marcus. To conclude with Doris V. Falk, "Lavinia's character adds a new dimension to the Hubbard Saga and her presence in the play means that some good blood has been brought into the Hubbard clan."[8]

The Bagtrys—Birdie Bagtry, her mother and her cousin, John Bagtry—fall a total contrast to the Hubbards. Because of their gentle nature they always hate Hubbard machinations. Birdie is portrayed as a girl of twenty with seedy clothes and frightened face.[9] Birdie is presented as the penniless daughter of the aristocratic Bagtry who is forced to come and ask Ben to arrange a loan to save the family plantation, Lionnet. She is unmarried and unable to sell her cotton and thus support those who work for her. She is a pathetic victim of fading aristocracy who tries her best to retain her family property.

John Bagtry, the cousin of Birdie, is an ex-Confederate Officer. He is essentially a man of honour, an officer and a gentleman, who was happy only during the war when he was in the army. He is loved by Regina, who plans to flee with him to Chicago. However, John's affair with Regina is beginning to pale at the end and all he wants now is to go to Brazil to fight in a war brewing there. At the end of the play, Ben enables him to leave Regina and go to Brazil. With only one desire to go to Brazil, John Bagtry is a burnt-out case, something like Chekhov's Ivanov, in his relation to the young and vital Regina.

An important feature of Hellman's art of characterization in *Another Part of the Forest* is her experimentation with moving towards a more internal examination of women. The three central women of the play—Lavinia, Birdie and young Regina—live more or less according to the dictates of men. Lavinia, consumed with guilt for not speaking out about her husband's lies and wrong-doings, gradually retreats to a world of fantasy. Birdie, a passive and vulnerable member of the dying aristocracy, is forced to marry Oscar to remain solvent. Even Regina, the most formidable woman, is made to please her father and then Ben, who marries her off to Horace Giddens, in spite of her liking John Bagtry. Whatever 'wholesale wickedness' is contrived among the Hubbards, Hellman shows how the social and economic powerlessness of women puts them at a disadvantage. This reveals Hellman's most realistic and objective portrayal of women in the play. She seems to be one with Virginia Woolf in suggesting that economic independence is absolutely necessary for the full flowering of woman's individuality and assertion of her position in society.

Like *The Little Foxes*, *Another Part of the Forest* is essentially a realistic play. Hellman writes the play as she sees the world, past or present. The connection between the drive for wealth and power and the surrender of conscience is genuinely complex. Greed and egotism raised to the level of social strategy are things that Hellman has observed at close quarters and portrayed in the play *Another Part of the Forest*.

Hellman has the unusual ability to choose themes ordinarily associated with tragedy and fit them into a familial context where the facts of tragedy are really the facts of life. As in Ibsen's *Ghosts*, the sins of the father are passed on to the son. From father to son, the evil is bequeathed as if it were a birthright. As G.J. Nathan observes, "Hellman is not working in symbols but in terms of sharp realism."[10]

Another Part of the Forest, like *The Little Foxes*, contains an unrelieved view of an evil universe. The play is socially relevant as it is meant to expose the evils of materialism in a competitive society. The basic historical social struggle against which the play of the Hubbard family is cast is that between the Old South and the New South, between agrarianism and the new order which desired to imitate the North for the purpose of moving the region into the modern world. From the beginning to the end of the play, the contrast is stated and reiterated by character after character in scene after scene.

The play chronicles, as Joseph Wood Krutch points out, the "decline of the Southern feudal aristocracy and the rise of the capitalist exploiter. There are no admirable characters because, by antecedent premise, there cannot be any. Dying aristocrats must be dim-witted and rising capitalists must be villainous because otherwise the dialectic process could not have taken place as it did."[11] Like Faulkner or Penn Warren and later Tennessee Williams, Hellman seems to know all too clearly the corruption hidden by neo-classical facades and romantic lies.

The realistic mode of the play is happily matched with its all-pervasive dramatic irony. The audience knows what Regina's real plans are, what the real deal Ben has made with Birdie, and what evidence Lavinia has to hang Marcus. Ben, for example, does not want Birdie to talk to Marcus about the loan. When Birdie says she would never talk business at a party, Ben replies sardonically: "Good breeding is very useful." (379) The audience also knows before Regina and Oscar that their plans will be thwarted.

The very structure of the play, like that of Shakespeare's *King Lear*, is fraught with boomerang irony. In the words of Katherine Lederer: "Had Marcus granted Lavinia's request, she would not have been present to be the instrument of his downfall. Had Marcus let Ben have the money to invest in coal, Ben would not have schemed to get it through Birdie, would not have been thwarted by 'Regina's trying to keep Bagtry from going to Brazil, would not have been ordered out of the house, and would not have gotten the information that gives him the upper hand. Regina's attempt to outwit Ben and keep Bagtry leads to her losing both Bagtry and Chicago and any freedom she had through her father's favouritism."[12] In Shakespeare's *Romeo and Juliet*, too, 'boomerang irony' operates on similar lines though in quite different situations.

Without fully grasping the satiric base and ironic mode of

the play, some critics have categorized *Another Part of the Forest* as a melodrama of social protest. For instance, George Jean Nathan thinks that Hellman had tried a "drama of hate and avarice in the Strindberg manner and had wound up with overwrought melodrama."[13] J.M. Brown feels that Hellman sets before us "the fun—the good, tingling almost freak-show fun—of her melodrama which comes from the wholesale villainy of her characters."[14] Leonard Unger observes: "*Another Part of the Forest* is melodrama employing a time-honoured combination: the family secret and the object by which it is revealed."[15] Some critics went even further and assumed that Hellman had tried to write a tragedy and fallen short into melodrama. This is made clear to us through what Hellman herself says in this regard in *Pentimento*:

> I believed that I could now make clear that I had meant the first play *The Little Foxes* as a kind of satire. I tried to do that in *Another Part of the Forest*, but what I thought funny or outrageous the critics thought sad, touching or plotty and melodramatic.[16]

Since Hellman is a social critic and a writer of melodrama, critics consider *Another Part of the Forest* as a melodramatic study of the rise of capitalism. Also the ironic detachment that crops up in the play, which is rare in American drama, has been viewed with some misgivings resulting in failure to get to the purpose and tone of the play. What we have to remember is that *The Little Foxes* and *Another Part of the Forest* are in the tradition of Ben Jonson's *Volpone* and *The Alchemist*. As Katherine Lederer points out, "Like *The Little Foxes*, *Another Part of the Forest*, from its title to its curtain, is not a melodrama; it is not a tragedy, failed or otherwise. It is an ironic detached comedy."[17]

It is interesting to note some similarities between Hellman's *Another Part of the Forest* and Faulkner's *Absalom, Absalom!* and Galsworthy's *Forsyte Saga*. Marcus Hubbard's futile attempt to establish himself as an aristocrat bears striking parallels to the efforts of Thomas Sutpen in Faulkner's *Absalom, Absalom!*, published three years before *Another Part of the Forest*. In both Hellman's play and Faulkner's novel, there are Greek tragic elements to portray a man who achieves great wealth through mysterious and suspicious means and launches a determined campaign to become an aristocrat. Both Faulkner's and Hellman's protagonists—Sutpen and Marcus—have vague, ineffectual, flighty wives who finally effect a kind of escape from painful reality in mental illness. There are also parallels between their daughters. Regina, like Judith Sutpen and Clytie, is strong-willed, although she does not share their moral strength. Both Marcus and Sutpen have two sons who, in different ways, prove their undoing.

The Hubbard family in *Another Part of the Forest* and *The Little Foxes* which shows signs of becoming a literary dynasty is comparable to Galsworthy's *The Forsyte Saga* (1921). Like Hellman, Galsworthy presents a vivid picture of the upper class people—the Forsytes—who have infinite love for property, social dignity, material wealth and power. As for the Hubbards, for the Forsytes what cannot be bought does not exist. The life of the emotions and the holiness of the heart's affections are as closed to them as the life of pure thought. Theirs is a life of making money.

To conclude, *Another Part of the Forest*, like *The Little Foxes*, is a strong and exciting play, artistically chronicling the greed and hatred in members of the Hubbard family. The greedy machinations of the Hubbards are followed with a cold eye as if watching a Brecht-like epic. With its tight plot, vivid characters, realistic flavour, ironic tinge and its caustic angry tone, *Another Part of the Forest* is more than just gripping theatre. It is one of the superb works of art in American drama, exploring deeply the origins of human evil with an understanding derived from psychoanalysis. In combination with *The Little Foxes*, it constitutes a unit which is, perhaps, Hellman's best contribution to the literature of the American theatre.

NOTES

1. C.W.E. Bigsby, "Lillian Hellman," *A Critical Introduction to Twentieth Century American Drama* (Cambridge University Press, 1982), p. 288.
2. David Sievers, *Freud on Broadway* (New York: Hermitage House, 1955), p. 284.
3. Joseph Wood Krutch, "Drama," *The Nation*, 163, No. 23, Dec. 7, 1946, p. 670.
4. David Sievers, p. 284.
5. Lillian Hellman, *Another Part of the Forest*, in *The Collected Plays* (Boston-Toronto: Little Brown, 1971), p. 395.
6. Sharon Friedman, "Feminism as Theme," *American Studies*, Vol. 25-26, 1984-85, p. 83.
7. In creating Lavinia, Hellman may have used something of her mother's vague but sincere religiosity as described in *An Unfinished Woman* and *Pentimento*.
8. D.V. Falk, *Lillian Hellman* (New York: Alfred & Knopf, 1978), p. 61.
9. Hellman's mother, Julia Newhouse, is said to be the model for Birdie both in *Another Part of the Forest* and *The Little Foxes*. See *Pentimento*, p. 80.
10. G.J. Nathan, *The Theatre Book of the Year 1946-1947* (New York, 1947), p. 202.
11. Joseph Wood Krutch, *Nation*, December 7, 1946, p. 171.
12. Katherine Lederer, *Lillian Hellman* (Boston: Twayne, 1979), p. 70.
13. G.J. Nathan, *Journal of America*, December 2, 1946, cited in Katherine Lederer, p. 71.
14. John Mason Brown, "Seeing Things," *Saturday Review*, December 14, 1946, p. 21.
15. Leonard Ungar, "Lillian Hellman," *American Writers*, Supplement I, Part I (New York: Charles Scribner's, 1964), p. 283.
16. Lillian Hellman, *Pentimento: A Book of Portraits* (Boston: Little, Brown, 1973), p. 163.
17. Katherine Lederer, p. 71.

Being Static without Motivation: *The Autumn Garden*

An autumn garden is one which by winter time will fade and not be a garden any more.

Lillian Hellman

The Autumn Garden (1951) is, perhaps, the most original play of Hellman. In many ways it marks a new stage in her writing. For the first time she renounces the presentation of her favourite topic—social criticism, in one form or another, and concerns herself with a human problem that is not bound to social conditions. Her old anger against evil and injustice in the early plays seems now to have become a general irritability and petulance towards human inadequacy. Money, while still prominent as in her earlier plays, is no longer such a dominant force and motivation. Considered an unusually introspective work in Hellman's canon, *The Autumn Garden* is the first of Hellman's specifically Southern studies which takes place in the present. The play also offers a broader and deeper view of her society and generation than any other play Hellman has written so far.

The Autumn Garden is, perhaps, the most maturely thought and the most scrupulously written play. Showing the definite influence of Anton Chekhov, the play concerns itself with a society that has become static without motivation and with individual persons who try to come to terms with what they have made, or failed to make of their own private lives.

Written in the years of the Sartre-Camus debates, *The Autumn Garden* seems to be an existential assertion of the need to acknowledge one's responsibility for creating one's own essence. Hellman seems to introduce a theme of nostalgia for a no-longer existent past and the individual's frustrating search for love and the meaning of life. Hellman's view is that a reasoned life without a definite outlook is not a life, but a burden and a horror. Hellman believes in decency, intelligence and will as opposed to moral inertia and irresponsibility. She believes that we must do our best, our human best. We must not fool ourselves or other people. We must strive to grow and we must be committed in the essential sense of the term.

The main theme of the play is the problem of facing old age, the summing up at the middle of one's life. *The Autumn Garden* studies the dangers of ageing and living upto one's reputation and, what is more, the awful unspoken suffering of those who cannot admit to what they love. The play relates itself to a group of middle-aged individuals vacationing on the gulf of Mexico, who discover the ramifications of the decisions and compromises they have made. Here are individuals who are stalemated and, unable to take positive action, waste their lives and wither away and come by various means to a realization of their plight.

The Autumn Garden is set in the Tuckerman house in a small town on the Gulf of Mexico, a hundred miles from New Orleans, in September 1949. In this boarding house, Hellman gathers a group of people who lack purpose, joy and love. It is autumn not only in terms of the season, but more crucially in the lives of many of those gathered in the modest guest house. They live in a world of illusion, of memories reconstructed to afford a convenient absolution for wasted lives. It is a world drained of truth and hence of a sense of moral responsibility.

The assembled characters have little dynamic connection with each other, except that each is in search of some kind of meaning for his empty life. They come to the summer home, where most of them have grown up, and reach the end of a summer season, and in their lives too. They bring with them the real past and that past coloured by memory and in the real present they lose their romantic futures.

As the curtain rises, representatives of all the major clusters—Mrs. Mary Ellis, her daughter-in-law, Carrie and her grandson Frederick; Benjman Griggs and his wife Rose Griggs; Edward Crossman, an alcoholic bank clerk; and Constance Tuckerman, the owner of the summer house, and her niece Sophie Tuckerman—are on stage. One set—Nick Denery and Nina Denery—is not present on the stage, and of course, others are waiting for the missing set to arrive. Constance Tuckerman, the owner, a plucky but romantic Southern lady who was left impoverished by her supposedly wealthy parents, has converted the family summer home into a boarding house. One of her most faithful summer boarders is Edward Crossman, a middle-aged intellectual, who was once in love with Constance and who now finds his chief solace in alcohol. Constance has a young niece, Sophie, daughter of her brother and his French wife. Sophie's father died during the war and Constance thought it her duty to rescue Sophie from poverty in a French village. Now Sophie helps her aunt with the work at the boarding house.

Sophie is engaged to Frederick Ellis, a young man who is staying at the Tuckerman house with his grandmother and his mother. The grandmother Mrs. Mary Ellis holds the family purse strings and knows the power of her wealth. She dominates her daughter-in-law Carrie who in turn dominates her son Frederick. The engagement of Frederick and Sophie is acknowledged between them to be a matter of convenience. Frederick will give Sophie financial security and she will give him a home and respectability. Carrie approves since she feels instinctively that Sophie is no rival. Frederick's real emotional interest, however, is in Payson, a male writer whose work he is editing and who has a dubious reputation. Some critics have called Frederick a 'passive-despondent' mother's boy, who is latently homosexual. But nobody in the play, except possibly his mother, considers the inclination to be latent. The Ellises—Grandmother, Mother and Frederick—are planning a trip to Europe, without Sophie. Frederick is determined to invite Payson to go as his guest.

The other regular summer boarders are General Benjman Griggs and his wife Rose. Rose is a comic character, pathetic but childish and silly. Her husband wants a divorce, and plans to leave her whether she divorces him or not. Griggs has his own Oedipal hang-ups. He had always wanted love from a serious woman like his mother. Rose boasts of the love affair she had when the General was away during the war. But Griggs is beyond caring. He just walks out.

Into this garden comes the serpent, Nick, and his wife Nina. Nick meddles with everybody's life and goes from one group to another making trouble. His only motive is to display his charm and use his power to manipulate others. He flirts with all the women, but when they begin to respond, protects himself against any commitment. He has been doing this for years. His wife, who sees through it, is sick of his meddling and philandering, but she cannot make up her mind to leave him.

Nick's first victim is Constance who was once in love with him. Nick had painted Constance's portrait twenty-three years ago. Now he cruelly persuades her to let him paint her again. His plan is to retrieve from her the original portrait and exhibit the two together. Nick dresses Constance in rags, and paints her as a sad, poverty-stricken, old woman. All the time he keeps up a lie to Constance that he really loved her when he married Nina, and still does but that Ned Crossman still loves her too and wants to marry her. Nick will not allow Constance to look at the new portrait of herself. Now he encourages her to fantasize about Crossman.

Nick then turns his beneficent attention to the Ellises. He informs Carrie that he had seen Fred in the travel agency, booking passage to Europe for Payson. Nick warns Carrie that Payson was involved in a 'filthy little scandal in Rome.' Carrie thanks him for the information and faces Frederick with it. He still insists on taking Payson with him. But his grandmother forces Carrie to tell Frederick that he can leave on the trip with Payson, but must 'make clear to his guest that his ten thousand a year ends today and will not begin again.' The threat works; Payson backs out of the trip if he has to pay his own way. Frederick is heart-broken.

Nick's wife, Nina, has been through this type of thing often before. He can never leave things alone. She says to him: "I can smell it, it's all around us. The flower like odor right before it becomes faded and heavy. It travels ahead of you, Nick, whenever you get most helpful, most loving and most lovable."[1] And she threatens to leave him as she has done before.

Nick has tampered also with Griggs' marriage. He comforts Rose by flirting with her. For his trouble he gains her confidence and the promise of a $5000 commission to paint a portrait of her homely niece. Rose is ill, is beginning to feel amorous toward Nick, and asks for his advice. He suggests her to go to a doctor—not to be cured, but to be certified that she is truly ill so that her husband will not leave her.

It is Nick's philandering and alcohol that brings the plot to a climax, and the characters to their senses. Nick has been drinking throughout the second act. He makes advances to Sophie, who is trying to get to sleep on the living-room sofa, then passes out on the couch before anything can happen. Sophie simply leaves him there and spends the night in a chair across the room. There is an uproar when the two are discovered by Mrs. Ellis and others in the morning. Everyone in that little town will hear the gossip and think that Nick has seduced Sophie. Sophie makes use of her advantage, and, in so doing, indirectly returns all the others to the reality of their situations.

Nick, himself, is out of the action. Now that he is in disgrace, Nina comes back to him and the truth about her is revealed. She needs to punish and be punished. Nick tells her: "You needed to look down on me, darling. . . . You like to—demean yourself." (557)

The Ellises try to persuade Sophie to go to Europe with them, but she refuses. Frederick has stopped moping about Payson, but Sophie knows, as does old Mrs. Ellis, that Frederick will always be his mother's boy. Sophie also knows that she must have another source of income now. From Nina she demands $5000. Otherwise she will spread the word that Nick seduced her. With the money she will be free to go back to Europe to help her mother.

As a result of Nick's meddling, all the characters are confronted with the truth about themselves. But their life-long patterns cannot be broken. Nick was right about Rose and Ben Griggs. When Ben knows that she is ill, he gives in to Rose's appeal that he takes care of her. For Ben, escape is not possible. His speech of self-insight, which was written by Dashiell Hammet, summarises the philosophy of the play. Ben says:

> There are no big moments you can reach unless you've a pile of smaller moments to stand on. That big hour of decision, the turning point in your life, the someday you've counted on when you'd suddenly wipe out your past mistakes, do the work you'd never done, think the way you'd never thought, have what you'd never had—it just doesn't come suddenly. You've trained yourself for it while you waited—or you've let it all run past you and frittered yourself away. I've frittered myself away, Crossman. (568-69)

Now it is Ned's and Constance's turn for self-knowledge. Ned faces the fact that he has wasted himself, has become a drunk, living in a room and passing the day until night when the bars are opened. This is not because Constance turned him down, as he once persuaded himself, but because he 'wanted it that way.'

Constance has decided that she wasted herself, too, waiting for Nick when she really wanted Ned Crossman all the time. She asks him to marry her but it is too late. He felt sorry that he had deluded her and himself into thinking that he was in love with her. The curtain falls on his declaration.

Crossman:	Sorry I fooled you and sorry I fooled myself. And I've never liked liars—least of all those who lie to themselves.
Constance:	Never mind. Most of us lie to ourselves. Never mind. (572)

The only two characters in the play who have not lied to themselves are the young and old realists who have acknowledged the value of money, Sophie and Mrs. Mary Ellis. Sophie is building her future by taking action in the present; the old lady built a triumphant past in the same way.

The resolution in *The Autumn Garden* is as inconclusive as

the lives of the characters have been. Nick and Nina are reunited, Griggs cannot leave his wife and even Crossman realises that he does not wish to marry Constance anymore. If the curtain opens on a grouping, it comes down on a house empty, visually, except for Constance and Crossman, who will soon be gone, and we are left reflectively looking at an empty house, to which summer will come no more. A searching wind has blown through it, scattering the characters before it.

Harold Clurman says that much more 'happens' in *The Autumn Garden* than in *The Little Foxes*; but that 'Hellman took care to make it seem less.' He says that "she not only wants a greater semblance to the casual flow of life, but is trying to say something about the norm of things."[2]

As regards the plot-structure of *The Autumn Garden*, Hellman is said to sacrifice it, since she lays emphasis on characters over plot in Chekhovian tradition. Critics generally feel that it is "loose in structure, bends easily but without breaking is fluid and far from being meagre, overflows with characters and situations."[3] Although Freudian interpretation can help to explain it, it cannot give the play the dynamic plot development which it lacks. Even Hellman's most perceptive critic Katherine Lederer opines: "What Hellman gives us is not really plot, but pattern."[4]

Nevertheless, there are also some critics like John Gassner who defend the plot-structure saying, "if a loss of dramatic voltage was apparent in *The Autumn Garden*, at the beginning of the decade it could be attributed to her experimentation with a relatively loose form of dramaturgy for the purpose of securing amplitude of characterization and giving a rueful account of enervation and failure in society."[5]

In Hellman's first six plays, the initial situation is presented in terms of some kind of problem and in some plays the first actors whom the audience sees and hears are servants behaving in the traditional opening scene fashion. But in *The Autumn Garden*, the opening is quite different. At the rise of curtain, there are six of the main persons of the play. They do not direct their conversation or their actions toward any one situation. Each is concerned with his or her own problems.

As in *Watch on the Rhine* and *Toys in the Attic*, Hellman uses the leisurely first act to establish atmosphere and the attitude she wishes the audience to take toward the characters and situation. Hellman uses sub-groupings, duets between characters to advance the action, that is to strip the characters of their illusions. Act II gives us Nick in action meddling in everyone's life. This meddling apparently gives rise to many sub-plots each contributing to the organic unity of the play. The structure of the play is anti-climactic. No one marries, no one dies and no one is moved to some horrendously final act. The use of a pattern of multiple characters demonstrating the same theme, leads once again to a play without a protagonist.

Hellman's artistry, however, appears more in character development. Her characterization shows a notable advance in subtlety as she views her people with more sympathy and less simple judgement. She sees her crisp characters "with a certain smiling asperity, an astringent, almost cruel clarity."[6]

Most of the characters in *The Autumn Garden* are 'deluded romantics.' They look backwards to find the mistakes of the past. They wander aimlessly following their inclinations, seeking to fathom the mysteries of their past lives and to discover solace in the present. However, for all their wavering in purpose and lack of self-knowledge, they have no blurred edges. They weigh so much, measure so much, the whole is the neat sum of the perceptible parts. This is the reason why Hellman is justly praised for her characterization.

The characters—Constance, Ned Crossman, Benjman Griggs, Rose Griggs, Carrie Ellis, Frederick Ellis, Nick Denery and Nina Denery—are ordinary, nice people, average to their class but in this sense, they are representative of far more of us than we care to believe. Hellman finds none of them bad, but in the light of their own sweet earnestness, rather silly. They are unwittingly self-condemned, even before they are socially condemned, because they are not intelligent in relation to any total human objective. They are idealists whose ideals are conventions and chimeras rather than goals. They will wither and disappear in a mist of empty sighs.

To examine the characters individually, Constance Tuckerman is presented as a victim of her own illusions. She is left impoverished by her parents and gets disillusioned with her love-affair. She indulges in self-deception. When Nick, her lover, who drew her portrait when she was young, requests her again to allow him to portray her at her present age, she takes an objection to it. She says: "I don't want to see myself now. I don't want to see all the changes. And I don't want other people to stand and talk about them. I don't want people to laugh at me or pity me." (509) Finally she realizes that her romantic notions about Nick are false, that her dreams for Sophie are false and that her old beauty is a beauty no longer. Some critics tend to make Constance a central character whose 'discoveries' have no resolution. But *The Autumn Garden* is a multiple character drama and no one can be the protagonist of the play.

Ned Crossman is a middle-aged intellectual. He is an alcoholic bank clerk who has supposedly been in love with Constance for years. Crossman is an ironist and sees through Nick's nature immediately. When Nick says: "We loved each other, so very much, Remember, Ned?" (506) Crossman replies that he doesn't "remember that much love." (506) But Crossman, with all his irony, "satisfies himself with 'understanding' everything except that he is wasting his life and that his 'honesty' has no object except to hide his own futility from himself."[7]

Benjman Griggs is a retired army general who allows himself to fall into domestic fetters in his destructive, stagnating relationship with his wife, Rose. Griggs knows what has come to be and will be. He even knows that there is no one person or outside force to blame. In the end when it becomes inevitable for him to keep his wife with him, he comes to recognise, with anguish and disappointment, that they can never break away to shape their lives in a constructive, fulfilling way.

Rose Griggs is a flirtatious, pathetically silly wife. She exists on social gabble and gossip. Gregariousness keeps her 'young' and 'gay'—two words she uses more than once in the play. Having no inner life, she lives off the lives of others. She flirts with

Nick and seeks his advice to show a doctor's certificate to her husband about her illness so that Ben will not force her for divorce. In the end, she too is stripped of her illusions when her presentation of illness turns out to be true.

Carrie Ellis, the mother of Frederick Ellis, is presented as a woman who is hasty in taking decision without any thinking. She is dominated by her mother-in-law, and in turn, she dominates her son, Frederick. With her mother-in-law's prompting, she even confronts her son with the threat of cutting the regular pocket-money. On the other hand, Frederick has no self-will and always depends on his mother and grandmother. He is so fond of Payson, a homosexual, that some critics find him to be a passive dependent.

Hellman, with her deep insight into human psychology, probes the motivations of a charming villain, Nick Denery. Like Rose Griggs, Nick lives off other people's emotions, although he is more active than her. He is an ironic catalyst. The play turns on Nick's awaited arrival and its consequences. Nick meddles with everybody's life and troubles them group by group. He deliberately manipulates other human beings for his own amusement. Nick's feeding off other's lives is revealed in the action of the play through his interaction with each sub-group of characters.

But there are critics who do not see Nick as a villain and harmful person. For instance, Harold Clurman feels: "the dilettante painter, an intellectual lightweight and universal flirt is actually less damaged than the intelligent Crossman, who has no object except to hide his own futility from himself."[8] Bigsby also defends Nick saying: "they are briefly shaken out of their protective illusions by the arrival of Nick, a failed artist who acts as a catalyst."[9] The arrival of Nick moves the action forward and activates reminiscences. Lederer observes, "more actively than similar Chekhov characters, Nick provokes the decisions and revelations that force the other characters into at least a momentary recognition of the waste in their lives."[10]

Nick is undoubtedly the most dominating character in the play. He meddles with the lives of others and shakes the other characters 'from their magnolias.' Nick tells Carrie that Fred is involved with a known homosexual. Her reaction causes Fred to learn that Payson has cared nothing for him. Nick tells Constance that Crossman has always loved her. Acting on this misinformation, Constance causes Crossman to face his own self-deception. Nick counsels Mrs. Griggs to see a heart specialist. Her visit forces her to face what she has suspected but has refused to acknowledge. The knowledge of her heart condition forces Griggs, in turn, to face the possibility that he never really wanted freedom, that he is all used up. Nick's drunken behaviour with Sophie precipitates another revelation for Constance, who not only sees Nick for the first time for what he truly is, but learns that Sophie has always wanted to go home. Sophie, in fact, benefits. Except Sophie, who is directly benefited by Nick's behaviour, all the other characters are profited indirectly by Nick.

Nick's wife, Nina Denery, is a rich woman and, although she sees through Nick's behaviour, she is compassionate enough to forgive him everytime. She threatens to leave him everytime he makes mess of others's lives but soon gets reconciled with him and even goes to the extent of repairing the damage he does. But, at last, when she tries to set right Sophie's life, Sophie teaches her a lesson, by boomeranging on her and demanding money. For the first time, Nina sees Nick's behaviour for what it is.

Mrs. Mary Ellis, the grandmother of Frederick, unlike other characters in the play, does not live in illusion. Bored with this panel of self-deceivers, Mrs. Ellis has a strong grasp of real issues of life—power, sensuality and money. She says: "I say to myself, one should have power, or give it over. But if one keeps it, it might as well be used, with as little mealymouthness as possible." (528) Like Granny in Albee's *American Dream*, who debunks myths by turning them back on the family, Mrs. Ellis is a straight shooter with a razor-sharp tongue who has built a solid financial empire for herself. She uses her power and her overheard words to create the situation that saves Sophie. Walter Kerr compares her to "the goddess Athena in a snapbrim fedora delivering her haymakers with aplomb."[11] She knows that it is easy to afford the luxury of morality when somebody else 'clips the coupons.' She readily admits that the happiest years of her life are those she has spent in solitude since her husband's death. She chides Nick for inflicting his bear hugs, friendly pats, and tiny bursts of passion: "One should have sensuality whole or not at all." (534) Mocking him as one of the 'touchers and leaners,' she asks if he doesn't find 'pecking at it ungratifying.' When Frederick discovers that his writer-friend Payson's real attraction to him is money, Mrs. Ellis orders him: "Take next week to be sad. A week's long enough to be sad in." (540) She knows well the system of patronage in which people like Fred, a professional proof reader and simp, must pay for the interest of people like Payson with their literary coteries. Like Lily Mortar's words, Mrs. Ellis's non-sequiturs describe candidly the parasitic relationships that surround her—Frederick and Carrie, Nick and Nina, Constance and Nick, Payson and Fred, Rose and the General.

Against these people, Hellman pits the half-European Sophie, a normal girl who wants only to do an honest job back in the grim environment of her native land, where things are not pretty or 'good,' but concrete, unromanticized, real. Hellman does not make a heroine of this girl. In fact, she makes her rather sharp, shrewd, decently matter-of-fact and not above taking advantage—with a certain humour-and-pride. Hellman, through the character of Sophie, contrasts American values with those of Europe.

Sophie, whose name means wisdom, is Constance's niece. She is a clear-eyed realist. She loses no illusions during the course of the play because she has no illusions to lose. When she comes to America, her values are already formed. She tells Constance: "I have not been happy and I cannot continue here. I cannot be what you have wished me to be, and I do not want the world you want for me. It is too late." (538) When Constance says that she was only thirteen when she came to America, Sophie replies: "I came from another world and in that world thirteen is not young." (538)

Sophie has a central dramatic role. She is the impoverished European niece, 'indentured' to the family for her cultural and social status. Like Mrs. Ellis, she is far too pragmatic to be arrested in self-deceptions. In the words of General Griggs at the end of the play, Sophie spends her life 'in training' for the big moment of her escape. Perpetually, verbally and morally, she piles up a lot of little moments to stand on. Seemingly tongue-tied and retiring when she first appears, in the course of the play, Sophie manages wry words for, and rare understanding of, the others' pretences. She knows that decisions are made only in order to speak about changing them. She says: "You know it is most difficult in another language. Everything in English sounds important. I get a headache from the strain of listening." And to Constance, she says: "I think perhaps you worry sometimes in order that you should not think." Sophie sees the social facade of Constance's romantic malingering: "Such a long, long time to stay nervous. Great love in tender natures . . . it always happens that way with ladies. For them it is once and not again. It is their good breeding that makes it so." (502-3)

Sophie admits the bargain she is striking with Frederick about marriage and knows the prevalent social code for women and knows also: "Somehow sex and money are simpler in French" (563) than in the indirect metaphors and oblique rhetoric employed by the Ellises and Denerys.

Sophie's refusal to take money from Nina unless it is called blackmail, not a charitable gift, is an important fact. Sophie does not suddenly change the character. She is not a blackmailer like the Count in *Watch on the Rhine*. She wants Nina and Nick, who have 'too many words for simple things' to face Nick's behaviour for what it is, not cute, boyish and charming but ugly. She realistically turns Nick's playful charm-seduction-disposal game back on him by demanding the exact commission he was to receive for doing a portrait of Rose Griggs's homely niece. Most significantly, the trade value of her bargain, that is, her role as marriage counsellor, is not lost on Sophie, when she says to Nina:

> You wish to be the kind lady who most honourably stays to discharge—within reason—her obligations. And who goes off, as she has gone off many other times, to make

> the reconciliation with her husband. How would you and Mr. Denery go on living without such incidents as me? I have been able to give you a second, or a twentieth honeymoon. (564)

To Sophie, the word 'blackmail' represents more than a way of calling something.

Sophie, in an inversion of Henry James, is a European who has learned to survive and adapt by facing realities as the Americans are unable to do. Walter Kerr, who understood Sophie well summed up her character: "The niece is, after all, a girl of spirit and considerable independence. She wants no favours, will accept nothing like charity. . . . The girl is both serious and wry."[12]

Thus, all the characters in *The Autumn Garden* except Frederick, Sophie and Mrs. Ellis, are middle-class Americans in the middle of the journeys of their lives. They start out to be one thing and end up another without realizing it. They delude themselves that some day they will be what they dream of being. They cling to a vanished youth and charm, like Nick and Mrs. Griggs, or they tell themselves that life will be different if their separate dreams come true. Griggs would have been a scholar. Constance, Nick's beloved and the inspiration for his painting, and Crossman would have been happily married.

In her introduction to *Six Plays*, Hellman says: "If I did not hope to grow, I would not hope to live."[13] The characters in *The Autumn Garden* have stopped growing. Nick is the perpetual amateur artist, the professional 'young man,' the eternally 'promising youth,' Rose Griggs still employs the flirtatiousness appropriate to a Southern debutante. They are all caught in repetitive patterns, although Nick and Rose refuse to recognise the repetition. They are what they have always been, what they will always be. The differences are in degree.

Like Chekhov's characters, Hellman's characters are also not changed permanently by the events of the play. Griggs and Rose will go on as before, so will the Ellises. Crossman will go on drinking. Nick will continue to make messes which Nina will clear up. Their reliving their past experiences does not change their future. The end of the play leaves one with the feeling that their past and their future are contained in their present and their present is ongoing. "They will do, do, do what they've done, done, done, before."[14] John Mason Brown says: "Hellman's characters in *The Autumn Garden* may be more numerous than necessary, but they are shrewdly observed by a wise woman."[15]

The superb characterization of Hellman allows her play *The Autumn Garden* to be far more realistic. The characters are based on real middle-class people whom we see around us in our daily life. And the setting of the boarding house, where these characters assemble, is reminiscent of the boarding house run by her aunts, Hannah and Jenny. Marvin Felhiem finds "the realism of *The Autumn Garden* to be the essence of human existence, not to the representation of life."[16] Hellman makes her point in the play that most people have insufficient will and here she does succeed in getting beyond her specific people to a more general and universal validity of her theme. Hellman has captured the universal human experience of the middle years. Sometimes in the middle years, everyman is awakened to what might have been and struggles to give his dreams a last choice.

The problems of the characters in *The Autumn Garden* are individual and personal. There is no cosmic background of war or politics, no ethical decisions to make as in *The Searching Wind*. "The context is supplied by Hellman's own text. As in the two plays about the Hubbards, she has drawn from her family memory book, but from later pages."[17] The concerns of these people are all of the kind of 'frivolous.' Harold Clurman thinks that Hellman, while writing the play *The Autumn Garden*, has in mind "feelings about most of us of the educated near-upper class. We are earnest, we yearn, but we are not serious, we have no clear purpose. We have no binding commitments to ourselves or to others. We are attached to nothing. The blunderers in Chekhov are brothers in our nobility even as in our abjectness. The characters in *The Autumn Garden* are our equals only in what we do not respect about ourselves."[18] Hellman's attitude to her characters in *The Autumn Garden*, and in turn to people who lack any purpose and are stalemated, is without any sympathy and almost cruel. The characters themselves perform the choral function of moral judgement on the action and the characters move from the world of realism into the world of art. For they are then not merely human beings but also become human symbols.

Although Hellman is a realist, she makes use of irony in order to drive home her theme effectively. And *The Autumn Garden* is not an exception. In this play, the number of people involved in repetitions of the central pattern further distances the audience, adding to the ironic effect. In ironic demonstration we do not empathize, we understand. As these individuals and groups move before us, we look for what they have in common, and we discover, as always in a Hellman play, that these people are defeated by their own 'life-lies' not by life.

Hellman uses dramatic irony in *The Autumn Garden*. There is an incongruity between things as the audience knows them really to be and things as they are believed to be by the characters. As G.C. Sedgewick says, "The ironic control that a spectator has over a play before him is a matter both of his superior knowledge and of his attitude of mind as evoked by this knowledge or by some other source of suggestion."[19] The audience's understanding of the dramatic action in *The Autumn Garden* is more involved than that of the characters. Although particular characters may report the results of offstage actions, the characters most affected by this information learn of it after the audience does. Fred, for example, learns after the audience of Nick's conversation with his mother about Payson. The audience learns, before Griggs, of his wife's visit to the heart-specialist. Not only does the audience have superior knowledge in this direct sense, but the spectators understand the import of the characters' speeches better than the characters themselves do. When people in *The Autumn Garden* talk, the truth is in what they don't say or in what they don't hear themselves and others say 'they talk past each other.'

The contrast between the reality of a situation and the illusions of the characters produces comic incongruity and 'irony of the incident.' All the characters in *The Autumn Garden*, except

Mrs. Ellis and Sophie, survive on illusion. Hellman makes Sophie, Mrs. Ellis and Crossman, to some extent, to control the audience's attitudes toward the other characters and their situations. In *The Autumn Garden*, Nick is the ironic catalyst and the play turns on Nick's awaited arrival and its consequences. The ironists Crossman and Gradma Ellis see through him immediately. Crossman, an observer whose detachment is shown not only in the tone and content of his dialogue, but in his usual physical isolation on the side porch, drink in hand. When Nick says that Constance sacrificed her life for her brother, Crossman says: "Nick is still a Southerner, with us every well-born lady sacrifices her life for something; a man, a house, sometimes a gardnia bush." (504) Crossman finally says of Nick ironically: "You're just exactly the way I remember you. And that I wouldn't have believed of any man." (505)

Mrs. Ellis, set apart by her age and wealth and an intelligent old lady who 'is broken and senile when she wishes to be broken and senile.' When Nick, bored and restless, asks Mrs. Ellis whether he will enjoy reading at her age, trying fruitlessly to divert Sophie from reading to Mrs. Ellis, she says ironically, "No Mr. Denery, if you haven't learned to read at your age, you won't learn at mine." (534) When Nick puts his hand on her shoulder, shrugging it off she mocks at him and says ironically: "One should have sensuality whole or not at all." (534) And Sophie, finally through her ironic way of meddling with Denerys, blackmails Nina Denery for $5000, the same money which Nick demanded for a painting. And she teaches a lesson to Nina that she cannot always clean the rubbish which her husband created.

To enhance the dramatic effect, Hellman, along with irony, also employs symbolism in *The Autumn Garden*. Prose can take on certain qualities of poetry, and certain poetic devices are available to the prose writer, particularly to the dramatists. Perhaps, the most significant of these is symbolism. In *The Autumn Garden*, the title adds a necessary symbolic note to the whole play. Hellman herself asserted in an interview: "An autumn garden is one which by winter time will fade and not be a garden any more. It's a chrysanthemum garden. The people in the play are coming into the winter of life."[20] So in *The Autumn Garden*, the symbolism inherent in title adds a poetic dimension to the play and thus the play becomes interesting.

The setting of the play also serves a symbolic purpose. The setting of *The Autumn Garden* contributes to the variety of the play. The setting is just as much a part of the structure as the character, the action and the purpose. The South becomes what it had been in her earlier work, a symbol of a world in which a supposed concern with history is in fact a profound desire to deny its force. The evil of the South, as she had hinted in the early plays, had lain precisely in its denial of the real and hence of the moral responsibility which it spawned.

The house of Constance Tuckerman serves a symbolic function, just as the houses of Madame Ranevsky do in *The Cherry Orchard*, of Sorin. in *The Seagull* and of the Prosorvos in *The Three Sisters*. It is the old home to which cling many memories but which has grown somewhat shabby with the passage of time. It is the autumn garden where flashes of brightness only emphasize the proximity of wintry sterility. As Bigsby observes, "It becomes an image of a hermiticism which stifles aspirations, an apt setting for those who have accepted their cultural and historical irrelevance."[21]

Like any other Hellman play, *The Autumn Garden* faced the controversy in the critics' opinion as to the generic category of this work. Many were intent on calling the play a Chekhovian comedy, some a Chekhovian tragedy, and some others a near tragedy derailed by too many central characters. For instance, Harold Clurman called the play "a Southern Comedy of Manners."[22] Katherine Lederer observed: "*The Autumn Garden* is a comedy, although Marvin Felheim wrote an essay about the Chekhovian elements in the play, treating it as a tragedy." Continuing her opinion that *The Autumn Garden* is a comedy, Lederer wrote: "*The Autumn Garden* is a comedy of anti-climax of denial of expectations. No one marries, no one dies, no one is moved to some horrendously final act. Audiences might have been happier had Constance and Ned agreed to marry but that would have violated the pattern."[23] And even Hellman herself agreed in an interview that "*The Autumn Garden* started as a sharp comedy."[24]

Although some more critics described the play as a comedy and spoke of the laughter and the wit in the dialogue, they also found the play pessimistic and depressing, an effect Hellman had not intended. Chekhov, too, has been called a pessimist. Hellman says of this charge, "I do not understand the pessimist theory. I know of no writer who even made it more clear that he believed in the future. There is every difference between sadness and despair."[25] Summing up Hellman's view, Harry Gilory wrote, "it [middle age] is a time of life when one has had a chance to try all one's capacities, felt the emotions of life, known love. One has the powers to enjoy life in any way that is preferred. At the same time, one can always have the additional pleasure of being reflective about experiences."[26]

Agreeing with Hellman and Harry Gilory, there are few critics who have seen optimism and compassion in the play. As for the optimism, Hellman said in a newspaper interview that "the characters in the play led empty lives, but that the play isn't meant to say that people can't do anything about such emptiness. It is meant to say the opposite—they can do a great deal with their lives"[27] that is, if one can start soon enough in their lives. The emphasis is on the view that at middle age, it is too late to do much about the life that has been wasted. So one can be optimistic about life if one is not like the people in the play. One should take hold of some clear commitment and should work towards it.

The play has a Chekhovian cast, appropriately set in the American South. They are upper middle-class people with their roots in money and traditions but caught in the essential tragedy, the tragedy of life. The truth is that the play is not Shakespearean, it is Chekhovian, a social drama, not a classical tragedy. As such, it has two necessary dialectical principles. First of all, it is a 'sharp comedy.' The world these people made for themselves would have to end in a whimper. The second significant point is that the dramatist foresees the end of this world, the artist-scientist hopes for a better one. The pity and terror are present but they are not for the single, noble individual like Hamlet or Lear, but it is spread out for all. Pity and terror have been democratized and made the proper subjects for prose.

So, in *The Autumn Garden*, as Marvin Felheim argues, "We have a kind of drama which makes for modern tragedy."[28] It is not merely psychological, nor sociological, but it is artistic and moral—and all in the Chekhovian sense. And so Hellman's movement in this direction is movement toward seriousness.

Although *The Autumn Garden* is an attempt at 'serious modern tragedy' looking at the number of characters and situations in it, many critics describe the play as having the density of a novel. If we pursue the analogy, we discover that Hellman's treatment of the action in *The Autumn Garden* differs from that of her earlier plays. Although she had in the past employed the 'messenger element' occasionally, in *The Autumn Garden* she employs this device often to tell us about events that a novel or a 'plotty' play would show us. On stage we see the inner life of the characters, the emotional results of the offstage events. We never meet Payson offstage; Frederick reads the proofs with him, buys him a ticket to Europe. Carrie confronts him offstage. He dismisses Frederick offstage. Sophie learns from Frederick that Payson is through with him, in an exchange we don't see. Ned and Nick have a drinking bout together offstage. The Ellises and Rose attend a party where Rose has a 'sinking spell.' Crossman, Griggs and Nina spend a whole Sunday together on a picnic. Rose visits her brother and a heart specialist.

Harold Clurman observes: "*The Autumn Garden* has the density of a big novel. The play is dense because Hellman has tried to construct it not along the usual lines of a cumulatively progressive single story, but as a compact tissue of life unravelled with the apparent casualness of ordinary behaviour."[29] By her own testimony, Hellman has always been more interested in novels than in plays and has always, with the exception of *The Children's Hour*, taken a novelistic view of her characters. *The Autumn Garden* is the culmination of earlier attempts at the novelistic technique, differing from them in the degree to which she perfected the technique of walking away from the big scene and giving us only the emotional effects of it.

It is interesting to note some similarities between Hellman's play, *The Autumn Garden* and Chekhov's *The Cherry Orchard.* As Felheim notices, "Probably no play of the American theatre is more Chekhovian than Miss Hellman's recent and most charming original drama—*The Autumn Garden.*"[30] *The Autumn Garden* marks Chekhov's influence on Hellman in the very title of the play at its closest which is reminiscent of Chekhov's title, *The Cherry Orchard. The Autumn Garden* is in many ways Chekhovian, though the resemblance lies in the ironic treatment.

The way in which characters, action and purpose are woven together in the play brings out the comparison between Chekhov's technique and of Hellman. The characters behave in a Chekhovian manner because Hellman lets them alone to act out their destinies regarding them only with love and understanding. The characters in both plays are involved in 'choral' action which becomes a comment upon the scene. As the voices of the characters rise and fall in *The Autumn Garden*, they give the impression that they are, themselves, comments upon the scene. David Sievers says, "*The Autumn Garden* is a muted, obscure play with the characters moving through decadence, sterility and emptiness as in Chekhov's world, but without the Russians' warmth and affection for his characters."[31] Even for Moody "the play is rich in Chekhovian qualities, yet she had missed a Chekhov essential . . . Chekhov loved them. In her play the glow of love was missing."[32] Hellman, unlike Chekhov, has more scorn than pity for these passive characters of *The Autumn Garden*.

It is customary for critics of Hellman's later plays to call them Chekhovian and to distinguish between the realism of Ibsen and that of Chekhov. Ibsen's realistic plays are strongly plotted around an idea or social problem. His characters oppose or react to each other in a series of confrontations towards a climax. Chekhov, on the other hand, emphasizes mood, not plot.

Critics call Hellman's later plays Chekhovian though any direct influence of Chekhov is hard to ascertain. Hellman published an edition of Chekhov's letters only after *The Autumn Garden*. As Bigsby observes, "For some critics, the play was Chekhovian rather than Ibsenesque to the degree that it presented the past as less a repository of concealed truths generating present tensions than a world of lost opportunities and betrayed vision. . . . Instead if Hellman is Chekhovian on the surface, beneath that she sees herself a moralist, as a voice calling people to the real world of pain."[33] Thus, *The Autumn Garden* presents an almost Chekhovian image of society, never denying the chaos through which we move, but by the subtlest shaping and selection creating an order within the chaos and lending meaning to experience.

Also, numerous technical similarities are visible—the de-emphasis of plot, the subtle personality clashes, the use of arrivals and departures, as is usual with Hellman, for emotional tensions. But the big difference is that she continues to stick to realism. According to John Mason Brown: "*The Autumn Garden* is unlike any of Lillian Hellman's previous works. . . . The mood, tone, the flavour, the point of view and hence the means employed are so different from those of *The Children's Hour*, *The Little Foxes*, *Watch on the Rhine*, *Another Part of the Forest*, that it is no overstatement to say a new Hellman has emerged. For the first time in her distinguished career, she has, so to speak turned her back on Ibsen, and moved into the camp of Chekhov."[34]

The Autumn Garden is a lucid, witty and incisive play. It is unquestionably the subtlest and most probing of Hellman's plays. It contains some half-dozen excellently drawn characters as well as some of the most incisive and revealing dialogue. The play also includes a measure of human sympathy. But at the same time, Hellman presents the hard doctrine that the little weaknesses we allow ourselves over the years pile up like calcium in the body.

The Autumn Garden is also a poignant, reflective drama as well as an ineffectual baffling and most psychoanalytic play. It is a sad play of the discovery of the lies on rationalization by which a group of people have lived only to learn in the autumn of life that their ego-defenses were only excuses for not doing what they could not or would not will. With profound psychoanalytic perception, Hellman has laid bare the dependency of humans upon each other and upon various rationalizations. Even though there is no single character with whom we can fully empathize, *The Autumn Garden* is a masterful attempt to look deep into tragic, empty lives which lacked only self-awareness.

The Autumn Garden marks a step forward in psychology for Hellman, enlarging her grasp of unconscious motivation beyond the sado-masochism which permeated the Hubbard plays. The theme of latent inversion, too, is suggested in a number of her plays. But as Sievers observes, "the task of bringing together in one play the complex and deeply perceived motives of *The Autumn Garden* and the superbly structured theatrical tension of *The Little Foxes* remains the task which Hellman's talents give promise of fulfilling."[35]

The Autumn Garden is certainly Hellman's most original, most probing, most mature play. Alan Downer says: "In a number of ways this is Hellman's most original play. Structurally it escapes the technical slickness which has been by turns the wonder and despair of her critics. Thematically it avoids the black and white values that have controlled the action of her earlier plays. Humanely it reveals the nature of our life, of our means of grace."[36] It is original in the sense that Hellman finds a way of relieving the sour taste of a stage prosecution with variety of characterization and some leavening of humour and pathos.

The Autumn Garden is most deftly constructed, the most scrupulously written play produced after a long time in the American theatre. And in Kerr's final judgement on *The Autumn Garden*, "the play itself emerges, at long last, as one of Hellman's very best."[37] So, as a playwright searching for a new means to express herself, Hellman is also sponsoring the need to re-evaluate the visual elements of the theatre in order to meet the demands of the increasing numbers of experimental styles.

NOTES

1. Lillian Hellman, *The Autumn Garden* in *The Collected Plays* (Boston, Toronto: Little, Brown, 1971), p. 524.

2. Harold Clurman, Review of *The Autumn Garden, Herald Tribune*, March 4, 1951.
3. Marvin Felheim, "*The Autumn Garden*: Mechanics and Dialects," *Modern Drama*, Vol. 3, No. 2, Sep. 1960, pp. 191-95.
4. Katherine Lederer, *Lillian Hellman* (Boston: Twayne, 1979), p. 85.
5. John Gassner, *Theatre at the Crossroads* (New York: Holt, Rinehart and Winston, 1960), p. 137.
6. Harold Clurman, "Review of *The Autumn Garden*." 1951.
7. Harold Clurman, *Lies Like Truth* (New York: Grove Press, London: Evergreen Books, 1958), pp. 47-49.
8. *Ibid.*
9. C.W.E Bigsby, "Lillian Hellman," *A Critical Introduction to Twentieth Century American Drama* (Cambridge University Press, 1982), p. 291.
10. Katherine Lederer, pp. 78-79.
11. Walter Kerr, "A Nearly Perfect Autumn Garden," *New York Times*, 28 November 1976, Sec. D, Col. 4. p. 42.
12. *Ibid.*
13. Lillian Hellman, "Introduction," *Six Plays* (New York: The Viking Press, 1958), p. xii.
14. Gershwin, cited in Katherine Lederer, p. 81.
15. John Mason Brown, *Saturday Review*, March 31, 1951, pp. 28-29.
16. Marvin Felheim, pp. 191-95.
17. Richard Moody, *Lillian Hellman: Playwright* (Bobbs-Merrill-Pegasus, 1974), p. 312.
18. Harold Clurman, *Lies Like Truth*, pp. 47-49.
19. G.C. Sedgewick, *Of Irony: Especially in Drama*, cited in Lederer, p. 81.
20. Richard G. Stern, "An Interview with Lillian Hellman," 1958, *Conversations with Lillian Hellman*, ed. Jackson R. Bryer (University Press of Missisisppi, 1986), p. 35.
21. C.W.E. Bigsby, p. 292.
22. Harold Clurman, *Time*, Vol. 57, Mar. 19, 1951.
23. Katherine Lederer, pp. 82-86.
24. Lillian Hellman, *Washington Times-Herald*, March 3, 1951.
25. Lillian Hellman, cited in Katherine Lederer, p. 83.
26. Harry Gilory, *New York Times*, Feb. 25, 1951.
27. Lillian Hellman, cited in Doris V. Falk, *Lillian Hellman* (New York: Alfred & Knopf, 1978), p. 83.
28. Marvin Felheim, pp. 191-95.

29. Harold Clurman, *Lies Like Truth*, pp. 47-49.
30. Marvin Felheim, pp. 191-95.
31. David Sievers, *Freud on Broadway* (New York: Hermitage House, 1955), p. 287.
32. Richard Moody, *Lillian Hellman: Playwright*, p. 372.
33. C.W.E. Bigsby, p. 291.
34. John Mason Brown, *Saturday Review*, pp. 28-29.
35. David Sievers, p. 289.
36. Alan Downer, *Fifty Years of American Drama, 1900-1950* (Chicago: Henry Regnery, 1951), p. 140.
37. Walter Kerr, *New York Times*, Nov. 28, 1976.

Destructive Springs of Love Relationships: *Toys in the Attic*

If I did not hope to grow, I would not hope to live.
Lillian Hellman

Toys in the Attic (1960) is Hellman's last original play which is most complex. We may also say that it is Hellman's most Freudian and mordant play. It ran for 556 performances, in popularity second only to *The Children's Hour*. It won the Drama Critics Circle Award for the best American play of the season. Small wonder if many of the critics wrote enthusiastic reviews for *Toys in the Attic*, calling it 'vivid' and 'vigorous.' It is less Chekhovian than *The Autumn Garden* and more like the earlier Hellman full of mystery and melodrama. Regarded by many critics as Hellman's finest work, *Toys in the Attic* achieves the magnitude and human revelation that have always been the mark of serious drama. It reflects the influence of Tennessee Williams's psychosexual dramatic terrain. It is a play that expresses a sympathy for its damaged characters which had hardly characterized her previous work.

Toys in the Attic is about two things—the effect of money on people's lives and illusions, and the destructive springs which run under the surface of love relationships. As in *The Autumn Garden*, Hellman has moved to a consideration of more private, intimate concerns, human emotions and motifs than materialism, secularism and amorality. She has advanced from human greed to human need which is a far more universalized theme than that found in her earlier works. If Hellman dramatizes the effects of wealth on the strong, in the Hubbard Plays, she portrays its impact on the weak—a wastrel brother and his doting sisters in *Toys in the Attic*. The Berniers of *Toys in the Attic*, like the

Hubbards, hanker for worldly comforts, but they are driven by love not by avarice and greed.

Toys in the Attic is a play about a man who deliberately squanders his fortune when he discovers his family's resentment to his new found wealth. Hellman clearly defines the universal theme that man enjoys dreaming of the unattainable but, once the goal is within reach, he finds it less desirable.

The play engages the individual psychologies of characters whose failure to understand themselves is the origin of their pain. Instead of presenting straightforward relationships of love or domination, she examines ambivalent ones of mutual dependency. It illuminates the injuries that people with time's help inflict upon each other in the name of security and love. Like the sad dreamers in *The Autumn Garden*, they are bound in a web of self-deception. The theme of the play thus relates the ideas presented in *The Autumn Garden* and repeats the motifs of human futility. But, at the same time, *Toys in the Attic* presents a fuller examination of the notion that individuals fashion their destinies by the accumulation of their acts and that dreams, which are inconsistent with these acts, are merely self-deceiving. Gradually the characters come to varying degrees of awareness of their self-delusions and go on their way with little hope for any future change.

Set in New Orleans, *Toys in the Attic* revolves around the obsessive and destructive relationship between spinster sisters—Arna and Carrie and their younger brother, Julian Berniers, whose sudden wealth and marriage to Lily threaten their domination of him. The scene is the Berniers home in New Orleans. Julian Berniers, an easygoing drifter, has been supported by his two doting spinster sisters. Julian, to the dismay of his sisters, had married a peculiar, immature young heiress, Lily Prine, whose mother, Albertine Prine, gave Julian ten thousand dollars as a wedding gift.

As the play opens, the Berniers sisters know Julian and Lily have returned to New Orleans from Chicago and think that he has probably lost his money. Julian brings Lily home and then showers Anna and Carrie with expensive gifts including two steamship tickets for Europe, a trip Anna and Carrie have always planned to take. Julian opens a large envelope filled with money and admits that he has been involved in a real estate deal and that half the cash is for his partner, whom he does not identify. Instead of being happy, Anna and Carrie are miserable for their happiness has always depended upon Julian's need for them.

Mrs. Albertine Prine, Lily's mother, has an affair with a Negro, Henry, whom Carrie calls Mrs. Prine's 'fancy man,' and who poses sometimes as her chauffeur, other times as her butler. Lily confesses to her mother that she had been happier after Julian had spent their wedding money and they were poor.

Bit by bit, the audience learns the details of the business deal. Julian has had an affair with Mrs. Charlotte Warkins, whose husband believes that she is white. Julian, however, has known that she is part coloured and is Henry's cousin. To escape her husband, who has treated her brutally, Mrs. Warkins has helped Julian to buy land which Mr. Warkins wanted. Julian has then resold the property to Mr. Warkins for a high profit, and Mrs. Warkins plans to use her share of the money to escape her husband.

The knowledge of Julian's past sexual relationship with Charlotte Warkins throws Carrie into a frenzy and heightens Lily's hysteria. Carrie over-hears Mrs. Prine and Henry discussing the business deal of Julian and Charlotte and after they leave she begins railing at Anna until Anna finally accuses Carrie of being vindictive because she has always had an incestuous desire for her brother. Carrie's feelings turn into hatred for her sister when Anna makes Carrie face the truth of her behaviour. She says: "You want to sleep with him and always have."[1] Much infuriated, Carrie quarrels with Anna, who decides she will go alone on a trip to Europe.

Lily's wild jealousy is intensified by the fact that Julian has been impotent since they have been in his sister's house. Whatever may be the clinical cause, Julian thinks that the emasculating presence of his sisters in the house is only a temporary condition. He loves Lily who had never threatened his manhood, and thinks that all will be well when he and Lily have gone away together, the house has been sold, and his sisters dispatched abroad. He goes happily off to wind up the transaction, to meet Charlotte and give her, her share of the money.

Carrie and Lily; who are left behind, are apprehensive. Lily feels that Julian may not come back to her at all. And Carrie thinks that he will leave with Lily. Anna determines that she will go to Europe without Carrie and makes her exit to pack. In the tense scene that follows, Carrie, still vehement, satisfies her jealousy by allowing Lily to believe—without actually saying so—that Julian married her for her money and will now leave her for Charlotte. With pathetic, childlike reasoning, Lily decides to beg Charlotte to give her one more year with Julian, and if he still loves Charlotte, after that she can have him. Carrie stands by while Lily telephones Cyrus Warkins to ask him to give her message to Charlotte. Lily reveals the whole story including the fact that Charlotte is of mixed blood. Carrie is silent except to supply the crucial information that Julian and Charlotte are now meeting at Sailor's lane near the depot. Warkins sends his men there, and they slash Charlotte on her face and beat Julian and snatch away the money. Julian limps home in a state of collapse. All his newfound confidence is gone. He cannot understand how he could have 'assed up' this simple deal.

Hellman distances us from the final scene because we have known about Lily's call to Warkins and because we are more interested in the effect of the beating on the other characters. Carrie is so happy that Julian says: "Why you start to purr at me?" (785) Albertine knows that Carrire will tell Julian that Lily telephoned Warkins and she tells Carrie to let her know first so that she can come for Lily. Henry had already said that he would not be there if that day comes.

The curtain closes on Anna who has been ready to make a definitive break with Carrie, picking up her valise to bring it back inside. Carrie has just bustled happily off to the store to get the ingredients for soup for Julian, who has 'always liked' soup. Carrie's parting line is Scarlet O'Hara's: "Tommorow's another day." (786)

The conclusion of the play reveals that there is a profound

pathos as well as an ironic judgement of petty lives in the misunderstandings and entanglements that produce the catastrophe. A man's life is ruined by his overprotective spinster sisters, one of whom has desired him incestuously. And the catastrophe that results in his disfigurement is brought about by his frantically jealous child-wife, who also wrecks her mother's life.

Hellman places the burden of evil on Lily as well as on Carrie, just as she does on all of the moral weaklings in her plays. Her judgement is summed up in the speech which Albertine considers to be her "good-bye present" to Lily: "The pure and the innocent often bring harm to themselves and those they love and, when they do, for some reason that I do not know, the injury is very great." (782)

There is plenty of 'love' in the play, but love is destructive when the giver and the recipient fail to understand its nature and their natures. And money is destructive when it forces the characters out of their comfortable, familiar life-lies, lies begun in their childhood, their origins forgotten like toys in an attic, but still subconsciously directing their behaviour. Money is the catalyst that alters the chain of human relationships because it forces the sisters to face the truth. They have always told themselves and Julian that life would have been different had they had money. But when once money comes to them, they face the truth of their real feelings.

Revelation of truth, which Hellman shows, is not always good and sometimes it is even ugly. It is this telling of the truth of Lily which causes her husband's injuries. It is this truth, which Anna tells Carrie, about her incestuous behaviour towards Julian, which arouses Carrie's anger. This is the reason why Albertine advises her daughter Lily not to tell the truth of her betrayal: "Can you have enough pity for him not to kill him with the truth." (785) But like O'Neill's *The Iceman Cometh*, *Toys in the Attic* is finally less concerned with debating the relative value of truth and illusion than with asserting the central need for compassion.

Toys in the Attic is a three-act play tightly constructed covering less than twenty-four hours. Like Shakespeare's *The Tem-*

pest, it is the only play of Hellman which follows the dramatic unities. It is constructed with all the rigidity and tensile strength of a steel girder. Nothing is superfluous. Every gesture contributes to the central action. Even the props, sets and costumes have an illustrative function. The characters are enmeshed together like the threads in a tapestry and the literate dialogue—even when it seems to wander—is always secretly rolling towards the inevitable catastrophe.

In the first act of the play, Hellman makes something of a mystery of how Julian contrives to become rich. The suspense is there until it reaches calamity in the second act. At the end of the second act, Hellman gets around more quickly in exposing the twisted nature of Carrie's devotion for her handsome brother, and the reasons for Anna's austere awareness of how a household survives by protective deception.

The play progresses steadily to its conclusion. A series of schemes, psychological abnormalities, sexual alliances and psychic experiences constitute the structure. The action of the play actually develops towards Carrie's recognition of her unspoken desires. The recognition comes in the crisis at the end of the second act when Anna confronts Carrie with her incestuous desire for Julian. The climax of the play is the accomplishment of Julian's ruin.

Although *Toys in the Attic* is a great success on the stage, as literature it appears to be too incomplete and elliptical on its own—without the knowledge of the Memoirs—*Pentimento* and *An Unfinished Woman*. This accounts for contradictory judgements of the play to which D.V. Falk draws our attention.[2] Some critics think that the first two acts are over-plotted whereas others say that they are dragged and nothing happens until act three.

However, critics like John Gassner and Richard Watts have positively responded to the ingenuity of the plot. The first act is undoubtedly somewhat slow and meandering, but as Gassner points out, "Hellman has prepared us suspensively with this act for the mounting passions and the tightly coiled spring of doom to be found in the rest of the play."[3] Yet another virtue of this sort of deliberate opening of the play is that "by the time you are faced with the secret horrors seething within them, you feel you know so much about all the characters that there is something inherently dramatic in the discovery that what you have seen is nothing more than their surfaces."[4]

Another reservation raised about the play by Kenneth Tynan is: "The trouble with *Toys in the Attic* is that it changes horses in midstream. It starts out as an inquiry into the moral consequences of wealth and ends up as a treatise on abnormal psychology. The more the focus narrows, the more the governing theme gets blurred."[5] But this criticism "indicates a misunderstanding of the play's true theme. Subject matter and plot are not necessarily to be identical with the theme, as one sees in an analysis of *Toys in the Attic*."[6] However, Richard Moody's view of Hellman's theme is more appropriate in defending Tynan's allegation. As he explains, "Hellman is less concerned with stirring our human sympathies than in exposing the quality of life as she saw it, in showing us the destructive powers of love, showing us that well-meaning souls can often inflict more harm than those possessed with evil."[7]

Toys in the Attic is to be appreciated not only for its skilful plot-construction but also for its superb art of characterization. After a sequence of plays in which character had been forced to serve symbolic purposes, *Toys in the Attic* engages the individual psychologies of characters whose failure to understand themselves is the origin of much of their pain. Like those in *The Autumn Garden*, the characters in *Toys in the Attic* muddle their way towards a kind of self-insight, but the truth about them turns out to be bizarre and the plot ends with a violent climax. In contrast to Hellman's active villains like the Hubbards and heroes like Kurt Muller, these characters are 'bystanders,' who do not intend evil or opposition to evil. They are hungry only for love, and their need for it, sometimes confused with the need for money, accomplishes their fate.

Always sharp at characterization, Hellman in *Toys in the Attic* has become more probing and wide-ranging about character. She seeks to expose the weaknesses of her characters in picturing their neurotic behaviour—the jealousy of the sisters, the sadistic trickery of the brother and the deranged helplessness of his bride. But the characters are original creations. They may not be lovable. They are believable and brutally alive. We may not find comfort in their company but we are fascinated by their pathetic neurotic lives. We cannot turn our eyes away from them.

When the individual characters are examined, we notice that Hellman uses a character contrast in the two sisters—Anna and Carrie. Carrie is a romantic who lives in her dreams. But Anna is a realist who is quiet and resigned to her life. What they have in common is their love for their brother, Julian. Lily, the child-heiress wife of Julian, brings the catastrophe to the plays in her love for Julian. Mrs. Albertine and her companion, Henry, are mysterious figures who seem to know everything about the characters and the situation but do not function within the plot. Like the chorus, they are intended to act as commentators.

Anna, the elder sister is more stoic and self-sacrificing than Carrie, the younger sister. The opening scene between Anna and Carrie gives a picture of the futility of their life and their meagre existence. Anna, the more sensible and honest of the two sisters, knows the fact that they have always lived for Julian. Anna, the most sympathetic character, though caught in her own self-sacrifice, expresses a clear insight into her own life. She is quiet, placid and is resigned to her life which is living for Julian as she herself declares to him: "You are our life." (736) Hellman's description of Anna as "a nice-looking woman, calm and quiet" (717) fits her temperament. When Julian showers Anna with expensive gifts, she is not happy, for her happiness has always depended on Julian's need for her. She is a stereotyped woman, whose life revolves round her loved ones. Anna is like a beacon of hope to Julian in the dark hours of his crisis.

Anna is the surrogate mother of Julian and Carrie to whom they turn for comfort and consolation. Sometimes, she wonders at her multiple role as mother and sister, as the bread-winner and servant of the household. At one such moment, she voices her opinion loudly: "I am a woman who has no place to go but I am going and after a while I'll ask myself why I took my mother's two children to be my own." (781) Her love for Julian is so intense and deep that she yearns to play the role of a grandmother. "I wanted to be around the children he will have. I wanted something nice to grow old for, I hold onto that and prayed for it." (771) But, her love for her brother is not self-demanding. It is the kind of love which makes both happy, the giver as well as the receiver.

Anna's sacrificial nature is evident in her strong sense of morality which overrides her personal wants. When she senses that Julian is in trouble, she is ready to help him, forgetting all her cherished dreams of going to Europe. She never complains and is never critical. She is always submissive and yielding. When Carrie finds faults with Julian for paying off the mortgage of the house which they hated, she supports Julian. Being angelic and kind, she is happy when everybody seeks her help, including Lily.

To the confused Lily who is not sure of her husband's love, Anna gives the solace and comfort she needs: "A woman who marries a man she loves should have a little more happiness from it and talk a little more sense." (772)

Anna is a realist who faces all the calamities boldly. The two sisters have self-revealing monologue and, on one such occasion, Anna confronts Carrie with the bitter truth of her incestuous love for Julian: "Don't know what's the matter don't you? You want him and always have. Years ago I used to be frightened and I would watch you and suffer for you." (766)

Throughout her life, Anna suffers, not for herself, but for her beloved brother and sister. Though Carrie gives the picture of the 'frail, the flutter, the soft,' it is Anna who fits in the description. It is Carrie who dominates her and Anna knows that Carrie has made her acquaintance at the office only to make them think that she controls Carrie's life. It is as if Carrie has created a role for Anna which she insists that Anna should play. Anna is a mere puppet in the hands of Carrie who is very dominating.

Anna is a quiet woman who finds salvation in life by living for others. Yet, in one rare moment, her regrets at having wasted her life for the sake of her brother dawns on her:

> The leaf came in the spring stayed nice on the branch until the winds would come to blow it in the snow. Mama said that in the little time of holding on, a woman had to make ready for the winter ground where she would lie the rest of her life. A leaf cannot rise from the ground and go back to the tree, remember that. I remembered it. But when it came, there was nothing I could. (769)

The play ends as Anna picking up her valise brings it back inside after cancelling the trip. Anna is once again back to her role of playing mother to the spoiled children, Carrie and Julian. According to Gassner, she has "a truly gratifying role as the older sister who combines an affectionate nature with a forbidding exterior." (483)

Carrie, the younger sister of Julian, is described by Hellman as a woman of thirty-eight, still pretty but the prettiness is wearing thin and tired. Like Anna, she too loves her brother Julian, but unlike Anna, she wants her brother's entire love to her only and she cannot imagine the scene of Julian's independence and caring for others. Carrie is a repressed woman, who by her childish desire to be pampered by Julian, becomes demonically possessive of him. She complains that he no longer pays attention to her since his marriage. She is hurt when his gifts seem inappropriate even though he bestows on her everything she claims she has always wanted—the mortgage to the house, a new piano, a trip to Europe. Her obsession has developed sub-consciously to the point of incest. When Anna is driven to telling her of this abnormality, she refuses to listen but seeks devastating revenge. She renounces her love for her sister and cruelly informs Lily of Julian's past relationships with other women. Her intention is to destroy Julian's marriage and bring him back to her alone. But the implications of her actions are more extensive than she knows. She destroys the illusory basis of her life with Anna and reinforces Julian's status as a dependent failure.

The germ of the character of Carrie is in Hellman's Cora in *Days to Come*. Carrie wants to wake up and find that it is 'years ago.' She wants to be able to go back to the 'secret place' with

Julian, where the children got away from the grown-ups, that is, from reality. She wants to repeat all the rituals developed in childhood when she says to Julian: "I can still jump, shall I jump and you will catch me." (730) Carrie cannot accept Julian's having sexual relations with any woman, perhaps not so much because she wants him for herself but because the act makes Julian a man, not a boy. Carrie is willing to destroy Julian—the human being to preserve her Julian-in-Never-never-land.

Although, Julian's life is ruined by Carrie, we cannot label Carrie as a 'destroyer' or a 'villain.' Hellman reveals that Carrie's fears about Julian's freedom are the forces which motivate her self-centred actions like jealousy towards Lily and other women. The expression of her fears forces her to discover that she and Anna have locked themselves away from the world, perhaps because they were frightened of saying or hearing more than they could stand. Hellman herself is in sympathy with Carrie's desperation, when she makes Carrie cry: "There are lives that are shut and should stay shut, you hear me, and people who should not talk about themselves, and that was us." (773)

The incontrovertible truth of Carrie is that she cannot change. She will not learn how to deal with her fears from this one episode in her life. As Hellman's vision of human behaviour allows, Carrie will remain as she is, finding other ways to carry on the pattern of her unrealized life. She resists the pattern of deception in the last speeches of the play after Julian has been beaten and Anna returns. She rejoices saying: "Let's be glad, nothing worse has happened. We're together, the three of us, that's all that matters." (786)

Carrie seems to be almost a neurotic. Although Carrie's desperation leads to the grim and final downfall of her brother, the misfortune she precipitates, however, is not a result of pre-determined malefaction on her part, but comes from a blind compulsion to protect her own neurotic needs. In fact, the real villians of the play are love in its most selfish aspects, and the human weakness to allow the need for it to consume others.

Allan Downer sums up her character when he says that Carrie is no capitalist dragon, no Satan lusting for revenge, no more incestuous than Ferdinand of *The Duchess of Malfi*. Nevertheless, she too is a victim: "She is what evil must always be the other side of good, tragic because she cannot know of her enslavement, because she can never have the opportunity to escape. She is the most memorable figure of a memorable work."[8]

The next important character in *Toys in the Attic* is Julian Berniers, the brother of Carrie and Anna. He is a good-looking young man who has been raised by his two doting older sisters. After several business failures, Julian marries Lily Prine, a rich young girl, whose mother, Albertine Prine, has given them $10,000 as a wedding gift. The couple moves to Chicago and Julian invests the money in a shoe factory which, like his previous ventures, fails. But he returns to New Orleans mysteriously wealthy, carrying $150,000 on his person. He and Lily arrive at the sisters' home laden with gifts. Julian is still a little boy with a little boy's dreams of making his big sisters proud of him. Julian is now in command. He has even taken it upon himself to write letters of resignation to his sisters' employers. Like Nick Denery in *The Autumn Garden*, he has something of the meddling do-gooder in him—another weak man married to a rich wife.

Julian's money, with his new independence, threatens to undermine the lives of all the women who claim to love him. Carrie, along with Lily, brings the calamity in his life by informing Mr. Warkins of Julian and Mrs. Warkins meeting in a park. Fully beaten by Mr. Warkins' people, Julian returns home bleeding and broken. Julian, after being brutally beaten and robbed as a result of Carrie's manipulations to hold onto him, eventually recognizes that he will always be weak and dependent.

Though we feel sorry to see Julian's toys shattered, our moral sensibilities are not really shocked. As Allan Downer succinctly puts it, "it is not that, like the hero of *Death of a Salesman* he had dreamed the wrong dream, that his values had been corrupted by a materialistic society. It is not that, like the heroes of whom Miller complains, he is the inadequate male who must yield to the all-powerful female. His life is shattered by a force unknown to the artist-sociologist or the artist-psychologist, by a force known only to the artist-moralist, the force of evil." (41-42)

Another fascinating character is Lily, the child wife of Julian. She is chronologically twenty-one, but mentally and emotionally about twelve. She is torn between satisfaction in the knowledge that her money had originally made Julian dependent on her, and fear that he might have wanted only her money. The thought that her mother might have sold her to Julian to get rid of her is intolerable, second only to her fear of losing him. Sometimes, she sounds like Hellman's Joan of Arc remembering her moments of glory. Lily is in a state of near hysteria throughout the play never knowing where she extends with either her mother or her husband. Her terror and her fanatical attempt to discover what she calls 'truth' accidentally bring about the catastrophe at the end of the play.

The next important character in the play is Albertine Prine, the wealthy but recluse mother of Lily. She is emotionally detached from her daughter yet engrossed in a love affair with her Negro chauffeur, Henry Simpson. She always finds her daughter a nuisance. In an interview, Hellman explains: "Albertine is a very rich lady, she's always wanted to get rid of her daughter. . . . So the marriage has delighted her. And she's the only one who feels sort of sorry for this poor bastard [Julian] and she'd like to see him keep the money and keep the girl for that matter."[9] A reviewer calls Albertine a character without a history. Along with Anna, she has the most literate, ironic, perceptive dialogue in the play. She seems to function primarily as a choral character, almost at times as a persona for Hellman when she says: "But I have bad news for you Julian—it's not simple being happy, and money doesn't seem to have much to do with it, although it has to do with other things more serious." (759) Using another favourite Hellman phrase 'in space,' Albertine says to Lily: "you have been saying you are sorry in space, for many years," (748) meaning without purpose or commitment. In the end, Albertine is clever enough to request Carrie, to inform her, before Carrie reveals to Julian about Lily's phone call, so that she can come and take her daughter Lily back to her home.

Henry, Albertine's lover, is perhaps the most shadowy and yet the most complex character. He is too worldly and dignified to be content to live in New Orleans or to be self-effacing when he poses as Albertine's chauffeur. In climactic scenes, however, Hellman emphasizes Henry's importance to the plot. His knowledge of the Negro quarters enables him to recover Lily's ring. When Mrs. Warkins is in danger, it is Henry whom Julian asks to help her. And it is Henry who tells Albertine that he must leave her home when Lily returns.

Although Mrs. Warkins never appears on the stage, Hellman makes her as real as any character on the stage. She is a woman whose hatred for an unscrupulous husband and desire to get away from him at all costs lead her into a shoddy scheme for mulcting him of a small fortune in exchange for a piece of swamp land he needs for one of his speculations. When we learn that she has been mutilated along with Julian by her racketeering husband's henchmen because he has been led to believe she is running away with Julian as her lover, our pity for her can be as considerable as if we had always known her.

The characters in *Toys in the Attic* do not change, and as Carrie says to Lily, "There are lives that are shut and should stay shut . . . and people who should not talk about ourselves, and that was us." (773) Carrie, as much a child as Lily, has made sure that Julian won't grow up. Anna, who knows better, will be forced to go on playing mother to the spoiled children. Mrs. Prine, who in a sense had sought her own escape from the sunlight of reality, must take responsibility for her strange daughter. And so they will live unhappily ever after.

All the characters in *Toys in the Attic* are based on real people. Readers of *Pentimento* and *An Unfinished Woman* know that the two sisters in *Toys in the Attic*, Anna and Carrie, derive in part from Hellman's aunts, Jenny and Hannah. The character of Julian is derived from Hellman's father. Like Julian, Hellman's father too failed in the shoe business because he was cheated by his partner. Hellman's father is also partly dependent on her sisters, if not fully like Julian. And the character of Lily, whom she intended to be 'not crazy but fey, and disjointed and sweet and lost, maybe a little of Hellman as a girl, a little of her mother. D.V. Falk writes: "The panic stricken jealousy—the fear of losing love, the ambivalence toward money and its power, the simplistic, fanatical allegiance to what she called 'truth'—all were stages in Hellman's own adolescence." (91) Mrs. Prine and her fancy man Henry are like Hellman's Aunt Lily and her chauffeur Peters. The memoirs contain other hints about other characters and situations in *Toys in the Attic*. We may say that many of them started out as toys in Hellman's own attic.

Hellman in *Toys in the Attic* takes a fresh and realistic view of the tie that binds husband and wife, brother and sister, mother and child. Conventionally its name is love and its end security and respect for the individual. But Hellman's dramatic method proceeds by balancing the opposing forces within a small group and by showing how the failure of an individual, a household group or a social set comes to reverberate throughout society. As a social thinker, moralist and a theatrical playwright, Hellman is concerned with human hypocrisy and evil in *Toys in the Attic*. She suggests social criticism in the off-stage character of Cyrus Warkins, the respectable businessman who uses thugs to beat up Julian and Mrs. Warkins, although even Cyrus's motivation may mix jealousy with outrage. Hellman creates a society of desperate beings, destroyed by the myths and values of their society and by the passions which lead them to betray one another as well as to reach out across the social barriers.

The principal virtue of *Toys in the Attic* is Hellman's use of irony. In order to show the harm wrought in the name of love by those who lack self-knowledge, Hellman uses the devices of irony with an ever-deepening skill. An arrival precipitates a change in the lives of the characters. There are characters who pass judgement on themselves. Much more obviously than in earlier plays, characters function as a chorus. Again, like any other ironic play, the title is symbolic and there is no single protagonist.

There is irony in the dialogues of the characters. For example, Mrs. Prine is ironic in her speech. Her words carry weight because they are ironic and seem to convey Hellman's ironic view of the other characters. Both the sisters, Anna and Carrie, have self-revealing monologues, which are ironic.

Then, the irony of character comes. In Carrie, Hellman gives us a character who assumes a role when dealing with others. We also discover that Anna and Carrie have reversed roles, or, perhaps more accurately, that Carrie has created a role for Anna, which she insists that Anna play.

The dramatic irony arises from characters who have insights other characters lack and thus speak ironically. Told that Julian has paid off the mortgage on the house, Carrie says: "Didn't he know we hated this house, always, always, always?" Anna replies, "You used to tell him how much we liked it, and the garden, and the street, and the memories of Mama and Papa." To this Carrie replies, "you know very well I said all that to keep him from being ashamed of the house." (741) Albertine says to Julian when he complains that no one is happy about the money: "Nobody should have cried about your good fortune, nobody should have been anything but happy." (756) At the end of the play, Julian still does not know who foiled his scheme. The audience, with its superior knowledge, knows that eventually he will find out and both sister and wife will lose him causing Albertine Prine in turn to lose Henry.

Hellman also employs 'boomerang irony' in the plot. Had Albertine not had her strange relationship with Henry, Carrie could not have learned that Mrs. Warkins was black. Had Lily not made her nightworld trip to the quarter when Julian could not have sex with her, Henry and Albertine might have been around to prevent Carrie's manipulation of Lily. The most traumatic boomerang is Julian's return with the money, forcing the recognition from all his women that they preferred him poor.

Another element found in ironic drama is the moment of false happiness before the catastrophe. In *Toys in the Attic*, not only is Julian's return with cancelled mortgage, new clothes and furniture and tickets to Europe a scene of false happiness in the usual ironic sense, we see the double irony that Julian is the only one made happy even at the moment, his women are dismayed. Julian is the agent of his own destruction. The gifts he brings, his new independence forces the others to act to recreate the old order. Ironically, then, the scene that might close a traditional comedy—the prodigal never-do-well returns a success and they all live happily ever after—is the beginning of the action in this play.

To enhance the dramatic effect, Hellman uses imagery in *Toys in the Attic.* In this play, the setting South becomes less a place than an image. It becomes an apt expression of unrealized hopes and misdirected passions. The social and racial divisions underscore a natural gulf between people who are locked inside their own myths, dreams and memories. The action takes place in a decaying mansion. The characters are trapped by circumstance. Hellman's gothic figures bear the marks of an experience of loss and failure. They cling together united by situation and a need which they dare not articulate. And these alliances generate the potential for pain and consolation alike.

Hellman's mastery of irony makes *Toys in the Attic* both character drama and a dark comedy. The theatre review of the play pointed out the weak points in the play, saying that "the play is melodramatic."[10] Adler said that "Hellman developed it as a fable about money, as startling as artificial, as theatrical, and as true as *The Pardoner's Tale.* This is not merely an attempt at realism, which fails because of the artificiality. A fable does not have to apologize for artificiality. . . . In *Toys in the Attic,* then, the genre is not problem play but fable and the technique is not realism but what might be called realism stylized."[11] But Hellman intended *Toys in the Attic* neither to be a fable nor a melodrama. Although the play ends with a melodramatic beating and knifing, the play is realistic. As Katherine Lederer says, "*Toys in the Attic* is a dark comedy. Hellman is interested in how the characters react when their bluffs are called about their dreams for the future." (99)

As in *The Autumn Garden*, Hellman makes an attempt to go beyond the realistic form, and to write a novelistic play. *Toys in the Attic* contains the descriptions of offstage events which could have been developed into full scenes. We are told about the way

Julian and Lily lived in Chicago, about Julian's big scene with Warkins, and about the scene in sailor's Alley when Julian and Mrs. Warkins are attacked and robbed by Warkins's thugs. And in addition we are given descriptions of scenes from the past, important because they affect the present and are more real to Carrie, at least, than the actual present. Carrie and Julian eating on the back steps, Julian giving food to Gus, winning marbles from Gus, and being forced to return them, Anna's eye operation, Julian's wedding—all these descriptions befit a novel.

It is interesting to draw some comparisons between Hellman's *Toys in the Attic* and Chekhov's *The Three Sisters*, Tennessee Williams's *Sweet Bird of Youth* and Lorraine Hansberry's *A Raisin in the Sun*.

Hellman's story *Toys in the Attic* bears various resemblances to the story of *The Three Sisters* although she has made it her own. In an article entitled "Miss Hellman's Two Sisters," Jacob Adler pointed out that Hellman has drawn much of the material for her play from Chekhov: "while Miss Hellman possibly returns to Ibsen's technique in *Toys in the Attic* her basic material comes from Chekhov's *The Three Sisters*." (43) The broad outlines of the connection are clear enough. In both plays, we find unhappy sisters and a brother who is a failure. In both plays, the family is of genteel origin and the sisters live in the family home which they all own in common. In both plays, the brother marries, against the wishes of his sisters, a silly woman who increases the family's stock of unhappiness. In both plays, the sisters want, or think they want to go somewhere else—Moscow and Europe, and finally discover that they never will. In both plays, money is blamed for a good deal but does not deserve all the blame. In both plays, an act of violence near the close returns the situation to a state of more or less equilibrium. Above all, both the plays convey the same meaning that in spite of moments of insight, the characters will continue as they were before because people are as they are: like Chekhov's Prozoroffs, the ultimate irony for the Berniers of Hellman is that there is no where else for them to be but where they are. Hellman has learned from Chekhov's work to take no sides, urge no actions or attitudes as she portrayed the Bernier sisters in a situation similar to that of the Prozoroff sisters.

There are also two basic differences between these two plays. One is in the action of the plot. The action of *The Three Sisters* covers a pèriod of almost four years whereas Hellman's *Toys in the Attic* is very tightly plotted and covers less than twenty-four hours. The other contrast is in the characters of both the plays. While in neither play do the characters want what they think they want, or even get it, in *Toys in the Attic* they come to realize the truth and in *The Three Sisters* they do not. It seems possible to say with Jacob H. Adler, "Miss Hellman takes a story from Chekhov in order to help herself toward qualities which have clearly not been easy for her to achieve—sympathy, objectivity and universal truth." (49)

Although Hellman strives for a Chekhovian complex of frustrated and unhappy people, her use of violence and sexuality brings her closer to Tennessee Williams. "*Toys in the Attic* also strays some distance into Tennessee Williams's territory."[12] With its portrait of a woman kept in thrall by her rich gangster or businessman husband, of two sisters who live a life dominated by the past, of a mentally damaged but sexually liberated young girl and of a man whose battle for success is constantly thwarted, it is close in spirit to *Sweet Bird of Youth*.

Toys in the Attic and Lorraine Hansberry's *A Ràisin in the Sun* have one basic plot similarity—business deals that result in a loss of money. Mr. Warkins hires hoodlums to rob Julian of his fortune. Walter Lee Younger in *A Raisin in the Sun* enters into a business deal with a shiftless character who absconds with the Youngers' insurance money. Both plays also involve dreams that come true, but the treatment of the theme differs. Hellman's characters are more content when their dreams are unattainable. Hansberry's characters are discontent until their dreams become reality.

There is also a Brechtian touch when Julian almost discovers the true nature of Carrie's love for him and then subsides into defeat and ignorance as if his own inner self didn't want the insecurity and trouble that would result from facing the true nature of his predicament. This may be how it usually happens in life but truthfulness's gain is drama's loss.

Toys in the Attic is one of Hellman's most hard-driving plays. Among her earlier works, only *The Little Foxes*, her masterpiece of the strenuous thirties, possesses as much penetration and dramatic vitality. In *Toys in the Attic*, Hellman has dealt with a number of unlovely or painful states of being, from incest to miscegenation and retardation. It is a play about the failure of growth through a failure to change, a dark and despairing playground on which eternal children wither and die. The play binds us to it with a cold, serpentine grace that is born of a clear head, a level eye and a fierce respect for the unchanging colour of the precisely used word.

Although Hellman's corresponding view of life is ironic and is trenchantly expressed, there is no gloating over human misery, no horror-mongering, no traffic with sensationalism. Unlike some well-known contemporary playwrights, Hellman has proved that she can deal with human failure without falling in love with it herself. She remains admirably sane in the midst of the ugliness and confusion she so unerringly exposes.

Small wonder, therefore, if *Toys in the Attic* has proved to be distinctly superior to the other new plays of the 1959-60. Hellman displays controlled artistry in this work. It contains excellent dialogue with vigour and virtuosity, incisive characterization and a mature understanding of human attitudes, relationships and drives.

Thus, a close study of *Toys in the Attic* reveals that Hellman's talents—her talent for original characterizations, her hard-headed knowledge of the intricacies of human relationships and her realism about the meanings of life—reap their rewards. Furthermore, Hellman "marshals her dramatic powers, tempers the melodramatic excesses, enriches her characters with a luminous, if neurotic, humanity and binds them tightly and irrevocably to their destructive course."[13] Thus, Hellman is able to combine all her earlier strengths with compassion, truth, detachment and dramatic power. It would be in fitness of things to conclude with Hellman's own view of the play: "I guess that's what the play says, too, to live by your own standards, even if you're going to be lonely and unpopular."[14]

NOTES

1. Lillian Hellman, *Toys in the Attic*, in *The Collected Plays* (Boston-Toronto: Little, Brown, 1971), p. 766.
2. See Doris Virginia Falk, *Lillian Hellman* (New York: Alfred & Knopf, 1978), p. 91.
3. John Gassner, *Dramatic Soundings* (New York: Crown, 1968), p. 483.
4. Richard Watts, *Post*, February 26, 1960.
5. Kenneth Tynan, *New Yorker*, March 5, 1960, p. 117.
6. Katherine Lederer, *Lillian Hellman* (Boston: Twayne, 1979), p. 94.
7. Richard Moody, *Lillian Hellman: Playwright* (Bobbs-Merrill-Peagasus, 1974), p. 372.
8. Allan S. Downer, *Recent American Drama* (Minneapolis: Lund Press, 1961), pp. 41-42.
9. Lillian Hellman, John Philips and Anne Hollander, "The Art of the Theatre, Lillian, An Interview," *Paris Review*, 33, Winter-Spring 1965, pp. 64-95.
10. "New Plays on Broadway," *Time*, Volume 75, March 7, 1960.
11. Jacob H. Adler, "Miss Hellman's Two Sisters," Mark W. Estrin, ed., *Critical Essays on Lillian Hellman* (Boston, Mass: G.K. Hall, 1989), p. 46.
12. C.W.E. Bigsby, "Lillian Hellman," *A Critical Introduction to Twentieth Century American Drama* (Cambridge University Press, 1982), p. 294.
13. Jacob H. Adler, *Educational Theatre Journal*, May 1963, p. 117.
14. Lillian Hellman, "An Interview," *New York Times*, Feb. 21, 1960.

Lillian Hellman's Achievement as a Dramatist

Beginning in an unprecedented economic dislocation and ending in a global war, the 1930s was a great period of revolution and resurgence. The economic, social and political conditions of the period, culminating in capitalistic societies greatly affected the literary world and brought about a radical change in the attitude of the writers towards life and literature. The social climate of the 1930s brought about a new awareness of the potentialities of the theatre. And the theatre became an active participant in the struggle to rouse a disheartened people to renewed optimism.

Social protest was in the air which was reflected in the creative thoughts of the time. With the awakening of the writers and the realization of their responsibility to society, commitment on the part of creative writers had come to assume new literary connotations. Dramatists all over the world started using the theatre as a powerful weapon to attack and purge the society of its evils. The result was a drama which pricked the conscience and stimulated the imagination of the people.

The American dramatists of the thirties looked longingly at the national theatres of Germany, France and Russia, seeking to enliven their own drama and to stimulate their own public demand for an American National Theatre, by emphasizing playwriting as an autonomous literary activity of the stage. The result was a plethora of dramatic works by native writers, in general, and John Howard Lawson, Elmer Rice, Maxwell Anderson and Clifford Odets in particular.

Stimulated to a great extent by the radical playwrights of Germany and also by a desire to spread the gospel of communism, as understood in Soviet Russia, the dramatists of the period began to use the stage as a pulpit to work out solutions to contemporary burning problems in terms of dramatic art. They were ultimately dedicated to the idea that drama should proclaim the brotherhood of man by exhibiting the evils of capitalism.

The play of 'social significance' was one of the outstanding phenomena of the 1930s. But most of those plays were "mechanical in structure, naive and unconvincing since nearly all of them were inspired rather by their authors's desire to protest against injustice or to plead for some new type of utopia than by an impulse to set forth, in terms of beauty or truth, some basic concept of human value, without argument and with no concern over its political effect."[1] As Lawson and other leftists continued to exhort Marxist philosophy through loosely constructed melodramas and Odets's plays became melancholy and flat without the tonic of his earlier commitment, the contemporary audiences and critics began to look for fresher themes and newer approaches to social problems. It is at this critical juncture that Lillian Hellman, who is rightly considered to be "America's number one woman playwright," entered the American theatre to fulfil the expectations of the audience and critics.

Supremely intelligent, respected by her peers, Lillian Hellman is one of the forces in the last forty years of American theatre. Her plays explore the human capacity for malice, the lure of power and money, and the dichotomy between individual interests and social consciousness. Emerging from the spirit of the consciousness—raising theatre projects and supported by the government in the 1930s, Hellman has earned a reputation as an outspoken writer whose primary concerns are moral and whose works dramatically embody her insight into the socio-economic causes behind the behaviour of her characters. She is favourably compared to Tennessee Williams for her powerful evocation of immorality in the Southern milieu.

Hellman is an early and impressive example of the independent woman. A pioneer women's liberationist, she took her chances among the men on Broadway. Her plays are bold efforts, indicative of social documents. They are problem plays, whose problems are no longer secrets. She is a tough woman who certainly does not relish the patronizing critical practice.

A woman of her time, Lillian Hellman is deeply stirred by all injustices and boldly speaks out against them. She does not hesitate to portray issues that draw upon the facts of her life as woman. But unlike Glaspell, Crothers and Hansberry, she does not present women's issues as the central focus of any of her plays. Though at times, Hellman's characterization of women appears harsh, she affords her audience the opportunity to explore the conditions of a woman's life which may lead to manipulating, possessive and emasculating behaviour.

Hellman is different not only from the women playwrights but also from the men playwrights of the period in her techniques and interpretation of social problems. Unlike Odets, she is not a 'theatre person,' an actor, who desperately wishes to write plays. Her desire to write drama is a curious one. Her true purpose in the theatre has been to ferret out truth in lives frittered away by aberrant lying obsessions. Her concern for social problems is clearly evident in her plays. And with considerable force, she attacks evils in society as well as the power of fascism. Combining her interests, she has produced tales of horror dealing with lesbianism, unnatural greed, and human degeneracy—tales in which she has imposed certain criticism against gossip, racial problems, and Southern prejudices.

Using both comic and melodramatic techniques, Hellman exposes the selfishness and the cruelty of man with a penetrating clarity and a highly theatrical, if sometimes melodramatic, effectiveness. Generally, her objectives may not be different from many writers of the thirties. But with superior artistry and more intense and controlled imagination, she has succeeded in suggesting a universality in her works.

Hellman has to her credit eight original plays, apart from four adaptations, all of them written on serious themes. The themes of her original plays are succinctly summarized by Ellen Moers in the following words: "All the plays are built around two consuming obsessions: family and capital. Capital is power, lust, hate, duty and destiny: Large public themes do of course march across the surface of Hellman's plays in step with her times like society's persecution of lesbians in *The Children's Hour*, class war and strike breaking in *Days to Come*, exploitation and corruption in the New South in *The Little Foxes* and *Another Part of the Forest*, the fight against Nazism in *Watch on the Rhine*, complicity of the rich liberal classes in the rise of World Fascism in *The Searching Wind*. Only in the two plays of the 1950s, in some ways the most interesting of all (*The Autumn Garden*, 1951 and *Toys in the Attic*, 1960), is the new stuff of family melodrama allowed to stand alone, without public trappings."[2]

Generally considered Hellman's best play, *The Children's Hour* is based on an actual British court case in which two headmistresses of a Scottish girls academy are falsely accused by a student of homosexual activity. Set at a private boarding school, *The Children's Hour* concerns a spoiled and mean-spirited girl, Mary Tilford, who seeks retribution for what she feels is unfair treatment by accusing two of her teachers of a lesbian affair. The play shocked many with its almost forbidden theme but suggested very clearly the bold quality of Hellman's approach to drama. It is neither a lesbian play nor even a play about lesbianism, as some critics think. As Hellman herself states, the play is really about a lie. It is both an engrossing drama and a serious study of abnormal psychology. It demonstrates the playwright's ability to weave tough-minded expressions of liberal social attitudes into a suspenseful plot.

Hellman's second play, *Days to Come*, unsuccessfully attempts to incorporate themes regarding the evolving character of labour unions and the conflicts between members of a family. The play presents a family of more or less well-intentioned Americans confronted by the problem of dealing with organised labour when their employees undertake a strike. Although Hellman says that the play is about individuals, most critics feel that the strike is the story and find no connection between the strike and the revelation of personal lives of the characters. The significance of the play lies in Hellman attempting to develop a theme common to all her plays—that the world we live in is the sum total of the acts of each individual in it. The play shows how ignorance, dishonesty and cowardice in personal lives affect social events.

Set in a small Southern town in 1900, Hellman's third play, *The Little Foxes* depicts greed and sibling rivalry among members of the affluent Hubbard family who seek to expand their wealth by exploiting the cheap labour force available in their community. The business venture turns into a catastrophic conflict between Ben Hubbard, Oscar, his brother, and their sister, Regina, as their quest for power and money results in double dealings, theft, blackmail and an act that is tantamount to murder. The play offers a scathing criticism of a class of people who manipulate society and the lives within it with a ruthless eye toward greater personal wealth and power. The play implicitly condemns the vindictiveness and rapacity of bourgeois society. Thus, the play is concerned with social degradation and moral decay as inescapable consequences of the inordinate appetite for money and power. It is a sombre study in the psychology of evil. *The Little Foxes* has received widespread acclaim for its strong characterization, tightly woven plot and spirited dialogue.

Watch on the Rhine, the fourth play, centres upon a family involved in the anti-Nazi movement. It is a vital, eloquent and compassionate play about an American family suddenly awakened to the danger threatening their liberty. It is the most human of all Hellman's plays, the warmest and, in some ways, the most understanding. The play asserts the necessity of struggle against both evil and the passivity of bystanders. The moral and political questions with which it deals continue to provoke us even today.

In her next play, *The Searching Wind*, Hellman advocates anti-fascist activity in an examination of well-meaning affluent Americans who fail to use their money and influence to halt the progress of Mussolini and Hitler. *The Searching Wind* is in a sense an extension of *Watch on the Rhine*. Hellman uses flashbacks to show us how the middle-aged characters arrived at their present plight and how their personal lives reflect and influence the world they live in. In this sense the play is reminiscent of *Days to Come*, making the point that the world is the sum total of each person's personal actions. However, many critics contend that the play's multiple scenes and numerous major characters divert audience from Hellman's thematic intentions. If *The Searching Wind* has plot problems and deficiencies in characterization, what saves the play is the dialogue which is crisp, clear, often witty and always intelligent.

In *Another Part of the Forest*, Hellman returns to the Hubbard family twenty years prior to the action of *The Little Foxes* in order to trace the origins of their obsession with money and power. The play centres on the family patriarch, Marcus Hubbard, a self-made man who becomes rich during the civil-war by charging outrageous sums for necessities. The elder son, Ben, blackmails Marcus into naming him the heir of the family business when he discovers his father's indirect involvement in the deaths of twenty seven confederate soldiers. Though not as successful as *The Little Foxes*, *Another Part of the Forest* has garnered praise for Hellman's insights into the sources of human behaviour.

Hellman's seventh play, *The Autumn Garden*, is concerned with a group of middle-aged individuals vacationing on the gulf of Mexico, who discover the ramifications of the decisions and compromises they have made. Considered an unusually introspective work in the Hellman canon, this play received positive reviews and drew comparisons to the works of Anton Chekhov for its emphasis on characterization and dialogue. *The Autumn Garden* is more individualized and technically experimental than Hellman's earlier plays. Unlike Hellman's other plays, it lays emphasis on character over plot. In a summer boarding house, a group of people who lack purpose, joy and love are gathered. Hellman's characterization shows a notable advance in subtlety as she views her people with more sympathy and less simple judgement.

Toys in the Attic is Hellman's last original play. It is less Chekhovian than *The Autumn Garden* and more like the earlier Hellman full of mystery and melodrama. It is a Southern Gothic piece revolving round the obsessive and destructive relationship between spinster sisters, Carrie and Anna, and their younger brother, Julian, whose sudden wealth and marriage threaten their domination of him. Like *The Autumn Garden*, *Toys in the Attic* basically looks at a family and shows the deceptions in the lives of the characters. Gradually, the characters come to varying degrees of awareness of their self-delusions and go on their way with little hope for any future change. The play progresses unsteadily towards its conclusion. A series of schemes, psychological abnormalities, sexual alliances and psychic experiences constitute the structure which is not without loose ends. The principal virtue of *Toys in the Attic* is Hellman's use of irony. Irony comes from characters who have insights other characters lack and they speak ironically. Hellman's mastery of irony makes *Toys in the Attic* both character drama and dark comedy. The play combines all Hellman's earlier virtues as a dramatist with compassion, truth, detachment and tremendous dramatic power.

Thus, Hellman, through her eight original plays, makes a significant contribution to the development of social drama in the 1930s. Her plays, though not purely Marxist, represent the highest achievement of the leftist writers in their organisation, communication of social awareness and intensive employment of thought. Like Odets, Hellman uses allegory to depict the struggle between good and evil, capital and labour, socialist and fascist. Like Odets, she writes with a conscious eye towards injustice, corruption, the allusiveness of material success and man's capacity for sadism and cruelty to his fellow-men.

Hellman's reputation as a dramatist rests on a handful of tightly-constructed plays skilfully depicting human perversity and evil. The destructive power of evil is a common theme in all her plays. However different the story, the place and the people, the theme of Hellman's plays is always the same, the struggle between good and active evil. It reveals Hellman's creative skill and technical equipment to approach a single goal from many angles and still to keep each separate line of approach clear, each story vivid. The single-minded devotion to her own idea of what is important and her ability to translate the idea into play, over and over again with an increasing power and persuasion, are Hellman's distinctive achievement.

Approached from another angle, Hellman's plays are all

about money. Her own complicated attitude towards money underlies all her work. Her major theatrical subject is money, how it is made, how it changes lives, what people will do to acquire it. Money and materialism are the main concerns of her characters and as they are greedy, they want more money. Money, in fact, is usually an additional shadow character in her plays, often the most important one. It can function symbolically but it also has a tangible, concrete, almost organic nature. In *Toys in the Attic*, for instance, money is stroked as if it were a domestic animal. Hellman sometimes seems to divide the world according to how people's loyalties and values are affected by money.

Although Hellman's plays are known for their revolutionary themes, they are traditional as far as the technique is concerned like Osborne's *Look Back in Anger* (1956). As a dramatist she is content to work within the traditional confines of the well-made play. Her plays are neatly structured with a good beginning, a good middle and a good end. The main character observes but does not affect the action though its violent consequences bring him to his recognition. The action and the participants in the action assume more importance than the plot and the main character. The participants in the action are named but not explored while the inactive main character is fully delineated. He is the only character who changes in the course of the play and the action exists for the single purpose of bringing him to awareness.

Hellman's plays follow a consistent dramatic pattern. The plot consists of a gradual awareness of a character who has refused to see or to act upon the objective facts of her life. The action, distinct from the plot, comprises a series of sensational events in the conflict of obviously good and evil forces which culminate in a physical or emotional violence.

Though Hellman is a social dramatist, her plays are not sociological dramas as some critics think them to be, for her characters are genuine individuals, not social symbols. The central interest in her plays is always on persons rather than on social ideas. Hellman writes in the tradition of Ibsen's *Hedda Gabler* rather than that of *A Doll's House* or *An Enemy of the People*. Like Odets, Hellman employs characters who reflect 'types.' But, her types are more oblique—the 'capitalist' might be a benevolent grandmother or the 'gangster-fascist' or might be a teenage girl. Hellman's heroes and heroines are invariably defeated by their own personal frailty or their own internal corruption rather than by social forces of economic determinism. Hellman uses economics and other social elements to create an abstract set of 'moral assumptions' and she attempts to dramatize the lives of human beings as they are played out against the backdrop of those assumptions.

Unlike other women playwrights like Ellen Glasgow, Hellman's interest is equally distributed between male and female characters. She often shows a remarkable knowledge of the male side of life and insight into masculine mentality. With the possible exception of Tennessee Willians, few male dramatists of her generation have demonstrated such a convincing understanding of the psychology of the opposite sex.

Interested in women and sensitive in depicting them, Hellman has always included major female characters in her plays. She uses their confrontations with both male characters and other female characters to provide the plays with energy and emotive power. Hellman's use of female characters is an important element of her dramatic method. She attempts to evaluate the variations in roles found in woman's social standing. The manner in which Hellman develops her female characters is consistently dramatic rather than novelistic.

To illustrate, in *The Little Foxes* Hellman approaches her women entirely from the outside. In *Another Part of the Forest*, she experiments in characterization moving towards a more internal examination of women. In *The Autumn Garden*, she perfects her power of internal characterization and in *Toys in the Attic*, she combines in expert balance the external approach and the internal approach. In her advanced perception of the role of woman in society, Hellman has drawn many women characters—from Regina, the vicious predator, to Alexandra the energetic new woman. In between these lie Hellman's other women—the trapped, destroyed, the well-intentioned but dangerous.

As a dramatic artist, Hellman adheres to the conventions of

dramatic realism. She is extremely realistic as an interpreter of South which provides the setting of four of her plays—*The Little Foxes*, *Another Part of the Forest*, *The Autumn Garden* and *Toys in the Attic*. Her theme in *The Little Foxes* and *Another Part of the Forest* is the rapaciousness of a family of rising Southerners. She contrasts them with the ruined aristocracy who cannot adapt themselves to changing conditions. Hellman's two plays contrast the loneliness of the falling and the rising Hubbards, illuminating on the two women, Birdie and Regina. Like Tennessee Williams's later plays, the later Hellman plays become more interesting, personal and autobiographical. For both, a shadowy plantation South reflects the present discontent. Though change is inevitable, the Southerners find the change painful. While Williams sees the enemy as time or fate, Hellman sees it as human evil. Yet, both share the common belief that strength of will and independence can triumph to some extent. As Nancy M. Tischler observes, "Hellman is the only woman playwright of prominence in modern American theatre history. Her portrayals of her native South are effective vignettes of 'home and frightening land.'"[3]

Hellman's plays are good examples of topical drama concerned with the realistic manifestations of good and evil in human character. Hellman believes that if one were a healthy person, morally and socially, she is assured of a rightful place in the social order. Hellman's dark world of those who triumph through a calculated disregard of moral values is as grim and full of pain as in the most extreme theatre of the absurd. Her plays are portraits of people and not of abstract symbols. Hellman's characters, though personally and morally responsible for their action, are always portrayed within a social framework, their motives rooted in social forces. Hellman is one of the first women to begin the social theatre. Along with Glaspell, she buried the romantic women characters beside the romantic women playwrights who created them.

Thus, Hellman's plays, like Ben Jonson's, are intensely realistic, reflecting as they do moral and social issues. Hellman's last plays reflect a deeper understanding of the complexities of human nature than her earlier works. The subtlety and elusiveness of her characterization add to the depth and texture of her works, suggesting an artistic maturity. Hellman does not present images of women as in any way stereotypical but tends to present them as fully defined individuals within complex social and psychological contexts. Hellman's plays are part of the wave of social criticism that permeated the theatre during the depression and the war years.

Hellman is essentially a playwright with a deep moral concern. In her hands, drama becomes a tool for conveying her moral concerns. She is strongly moral and writes with a righteous indignation. She is greatly concerned with evil in society. Her plays are, in a sense, studies in evil. The problem of good and evil is basic to all Hellman's work. In all her plays, the well-intentioned are destroyed by the 'little foxes' who are always around to 'eat the earth.'

Politically, Hellman is a liberal, an anti-Nazi and an anti-fascist who believes more in the rights of the working man than in any other rights. In spite of her bias, her plays are never didactic. Although there is implicit anti-capitalism in *The Little Foxes* and explicit anti-fascism in *Watch on the Rhine*, Hellman has always been most concerned with personal morality. Despite her obvious concern with social evil, Hellman, more often than not, seems to be pre-occupied with abstract evil, even to the point of caricature as in *Another Part of the Forest* or she goes out of her way to provide acres of psychological motivation as in *Toys in the Attic*. For her, however, psychological determinism, as *The Autumn Garden* shows, is never an excuse. Always a moralist, the playwright is usually intent on pointing a critical finger not only at the eaters of the earth, but at those who, in Addie's words in *The Little Foxes*, 'stand and watch them do it.'

Many of Hellman's plays explore the corruptive nature of evil and the decay of morally deficient characters. She uses allegory to depict the struggle between good and evil, capital and labour, socialist and fascist. She writes with a conscious eye towards injustice, corruption, the elusiveness of material success and man's capacity for sadism and cruelty to his fellowmen. The world of Hellman family is as violent and dramatic as a summer thunderstorm, but just as dry and airless and it is absolutely sealed off from strangers. In each play, someone lives dangerously, lives a lie, comes to a turning in the road and risks truth-telling. The truth is revealed and the evil is exposed.

Thus, Hellman's plays, which are well-made, are redeemed from commercialism by their strong commitment. Her moral message is organically part of her artistic structure and characterization. She constantly makes the point, equally applicable to private and public affairs, that it is immoral to remain passive when evil is being done. She believes that clear moral message "is only a mistake when it fails to achieve its purpose, and I would rather make the attempt, and fail, than fail to make the attempt."[4] Hellman's works, like her life, consistently demonstrate responsibility, courage and integrity.

Hellman's moral vision, it must be noted, is inseparable from her ironic vision and voice. Though obviously more overt in the memoirs—*An Unfinished Woman* (1969), *Pentimento* (1973) and *The Scoundrel Time* (1976)—her ironic vision is all-pervasive in her plays. And as Wayne Booth observes, "as soon as an ironic voice has been used to any extent in any work of any kind readers inevitably begin to take interest and pleasure in that voice—in the task it assigns and the qualities it provides; it thus becomes part of whatever is seen as the controlling context."[5] A careful reading of her plays reveals that those generally considered her best—*The Little Foxes*, *The Autumn Garden*, *Toys in the Attic*, *Watch on the Rhine*, *Another Part of the Forest*—are the most fully ironic. Readers and audiences with predilection for irony can hopefully turn to Lillian Hellman, the way they turn to Jane Austen and R.K. Narayan for an ironic vision of life trenchantly expressed.

In spite of her solid contribution to the growth and development of American drama, Hellman is often criticized for her artful contrivance of 'well-made play,' for her use of artificial melodramatic techniques to achieve the thrilling climaxes in her plays, and for her rhetorical curtain speeches. Critics like Jacob Adler and Barret H. Clark, who have tried to reduce all her plots and characters to repeated formulas and types, think that Hellman's plays are too well-made, depending as they do upon the careful structuring of events to create suspense.[6] They are of the opinion that "the plays, whose effects are contrived, whose threads are knit tighter than the threads in life do not convince."[7]

This charge is levelled at much of Hellman's work, and her answer is always to the effect that drama as a form demands contrivance, and that it does not matter if the play is contrived, as long as it is convincing. For, as Hellman says,

> the stage is a tight unbending, unfluid, meagre form in which to write . . . [The author] has three walls of a theatre and he has begun his pretence with the always rather comic notion that the audience is the fourth wall. He must pretend and he must represent. And if there is something vaguely awry, for me, about the pretence of representation . . . it is not that I wish to deny to other writers their variations of the form, but that, for me, the realistic form has interested me most.[8]

And, as to 'well-madeness' the theatre itself is a trick, according to Hellman, and demands that the playwright 'trick up the scene.'

The convincing well-madeness of a play can be illustrated through *The Children's Hour* and *The Little Foxes* which are widely regarded as Hellman's best plays. Both are well-made plays but neither has any action or character which does not contribute directly to the unfolding of the central incident. Once the initial situation has been established, the whole movement of the plays is direct and without embellishment toward the climax. The contrivances in both the plays are theatrically convincing and true to dramatic art.

As regards the charge of melodrama, the term is frequently used in a derogatory fashion to suggest that a playwright attempted tragedy and failed to achieve the necessary insight of a character development. Critics like Joseph Wood Krutch, Bigsby and William T. Going feel that Hellman can save her plays from an indiscriminate labelling of melodrama by avoiding happy endings.[9] Lillian Hellman, as a moral writer, wanting always to emphasize the consequences of evil as well as the distortions of human character that are the cause of evil, defends herself saying:

> I think the word melodrama, in our time, has come to be used in an almost illiterate manner. By definition it is a violent dramatic piece, with a happy ending. But I think we can add that it uses its violence for no purpose, to point no moral, to say nothing in say—nothing's worse sense. But when violence is actually the needed stuff of the work and comes toward a large enough and, it has been and always will be in the good writer's field. There is a needed return to the correct use of the word melodrama. It is only then the critic will be able to find out whether a writer justifies his use of violence, and to scale him against those who have used it.[10]

Properly understood, melodrama, through an exciting adventure which aims at thrilling the audience, is a heart-touching ordeal. It differs from the older American melodrama in the modern dramatist's attempt to be more subtle, more realistic, and, perhaps, more truthful.

From her able defence of the alleged charges of well-madeness and melodrama, it is clear that few women writers in the theatre have shown the strength and determination of Hellman. In both her life and work, she has demonstrated extraordinary power and integrity of ideas. She wishes to set right a 'system' grievously out of order through her plays. In an era that largely featured lighthearted romantic plays and drawing-room comedies, Hellman's preference for confronting more complex issues of modern society earned her the reputation as an innovative contributor to the American theatre and the foremost woman playwright in the United States.

Hellman is not a specialist in abnormal psychology or in the Marxian interpretation of society. She is a specialist in hate and frustration, a student of helpless rage, an articulator of inarticulate loathings. Although Ibsen, Chekhov and even Strindberg have been mentioned as possible influences on Hellman, she is fascinated by her own hatred of something. She is never a copyist. She has found her own way of making her own comment upon the American scene.

Hellman is a progressive writer and excels at contrivances, big scenes and sulphurous melodramatics. She writes with a fervour as a person to whom ideas and causes came naturally. The protest in her voice is strong. It is as characteristic of her as the energy of her attack or the neatness of her planning.

Hellman has no need of an entourage. Her plays are models of dramaturgy and worthy of revival. They are realistic and tightly constructed, reflecting moral and social issues. Her last plays reflect a deeper understanding of the complexities of human nature than her earlier works. The subtlety and elusiveness of her characterization add to the depth and texture of her works, suggesting an artistic maturity. Stylistically, Hellman's drama is noteworthy for its sophistication and polish and for its adroitly vernacular dialogue, for its unerring accuracy in transcribing the manners of diverse cultures from the small Southern town to the diplomatic circles of pre-war Rome.

In spite of its obvious intelligence, her drama is easily comprehensible to the ordinary audience, a quality which has enabled her to achieve an impressive box-office success. As John Heresy observes, her "plays are real classics of the theatre of our time,"[11] because "she constructs a play as if it were a temple, working slowly from foundation to roof."[12] It is art in the Aristotelian sense of the word—skill, craft, technique—that characterizes Hellman's work. Her work is a part of the wave of social criticism that permeated the theatre during the depression and the war years. Small wonder, therefore, if Rabkin writes that Hellman commands a technique which can "survive abrupt changes in the winds of doctrine."[13]

Hellman's plays project, beyond those of her contemporaries, the pungency, the ferocity and the sense of righteous indignation that have come to seem the very feel of the 1930s. As Barret Clark notes, she has "pretty well mastered the tools that every dramatist must use in order to gain the attention of the public. She is conscious of the limitations of the drama medium, and she has found at moments how to make the best of them."[14] Hellman is an impressive dramatist of the 30s, by virtue of her avoidance of the easy answer.

Hellman's plays have a life outside the context of the Depression years. They remind us not so much of Tennessee Williams or Arthur Miller but of a contemporary playwright like Neil Simon. Like him, Hellman is a thorough professional and concocts plays that maintain interest and quicken the pulse. If Simon is more entertaining, Hellman is more earnest, and more apparently engaged with important matters. They hold a mirror up not so much to man as to the needs of the Broadway audience.

Hellman's plays, as Sam Smiley states, while not purely Marxist, represent "the highest achievements of the leftist writers in their organisation, communication of social awareness, and intensive employment of thought."[15] The theme of class struggle is seen in Hellman's plays also, but her class struggle differs from that of typical Marxist writers, as she emphasizes social injustice, rather than class exploitation, personal rather than political or economic corruption, and a desire for understanding rather than revolution.

To conclude, Hellman has a dramatic mind, an eye for character, a fundamental strength and a complete and unremitting integrity that are rare among the native playwrights of her sex. Her creative skill and technical equipment are praiseworthy. What is more, she is adept at characterization and dialogue. Her skill in creating first-rate acting plays makes her well-made melodramas far more exciting on stage than on page. A single-minded devotion to the requirements of dramatic art, an extraordinary ability to translate her ideas into plays with an increasing power and persuasion, an ability for a superb portrayal of good and evil in life, use of melodramatic devices to dramatise social problems and, above all, an impeccable sense of morality are Hellman's distinctive achievement as a dramatist.

NOTES

1. Barret H. Clark, "Lillian Hellman," *College English*, Vol. 6, No. 3, Dec. 1944. pp. 127-33.
2. Ellen Moers, 'Review,' 'Family Theatre,' *Commentary*, Sep. 1972, p. 96.
3. Nancy M. Tischler, *The American South*, ed. Louis Rubin (New York: Dolphin Books, Doubleday, 1961), p. 349.
4. Lillian Hellman, "The Playwright," *The Passionate Playgoer*, ed. George Oppenheimer (New York: Viking Press, 1958), pp. 296-97.
5. Wayne Booth, *A Rhetoric of Irony* (Chicago, 1974), p. 176.
6. See Jacob H. Adler, "Miss Hellman's *Two Sisters*," *Educational Theatre Journal*, 15, May 1963, pp. 112-17.
7. Lillian Hellman, "The Playwright," pp. 296-97.
8. *Ibid.*
9. See Joseph Wood Krutch, *Nation*, December 26, 1936, pp. 769-70. C.W.E. Bigsby "Lillian Hellman," *A Critical Introduction to Twentieth Century American Drama* (Cambridge University Press, 1982), p. 280. William T. Going, "Essays on Alabama Literature," *Prestons and Hubbards* (New York: Crown, 1970), p. 152.
10. Lillian Hellman, "The Playwright," *The Passionate Playgoer.*
11. John Heresy, "Lillian Hellman," *New Republic*, September 18, 1976, pp. 25-27.
12. Leonard Ungar, *American Writers*, Supplement I, Part I (New York: Charles Scribner's, 1964), p. 297.
13. Gerald Rabkin, *Drama and Commitment* (Bloomington: Indiana University Press, 1964), p. 170.
14. Barret H. Clark, *Lillian Hellman*, pp. 127-33.
15. Sam Smiley, *The Drama of Attack* (Columbia: University of Missouri Press, 1972), p. 59.